LIBER SIGILLUM
Of the Lords Who Wander

Liber Sigillum
Of the Lords Who Wander

Gary St. M. Nottingham
INTRODUCTION BY BENJAMIN TURALE

PUBLISHED BY AVALONIA
WWW.AVALONIABOOKS.COM

Published by Avalonia

BM Avalonia
London
WC1N 3XX
England, UK
www.avaloniabooks.com

LIBER SIGILLUM
OF THE LORDS WHO WANDER

Copyright © Gary St. M. Nottingham, 2020

ISBN: 978-1-905297-86-3 (paperback)

First edition, February 2021

Design by Satori

Cover art: Seven planets personified (ff.56-66 Lullius (R.). Alphabets. Extracts from "Practica", etc: f66r; 1543). Wellcome Collection. Attribution 4.0 International (CC BY 4.0).

Illustrations and photographs throughout this volume © as credited; otherwise © the author.

British Library Cataloguing in Publication Data. A catalogue record for this book is available from the British Library.

All rights reserved. No part of this publication may be reproduced or utilized in any form or by any means, electronic or mechanical, including photocopying, microfilm, recording, or by any information storage and retrieval system, or used in another book, without written permission from the author, with the exception of brief quotations in reviews or articles where appropriate credit is given to the copyright holder.

Every effort has been made to credit material, and to obtain permission from copyright holders for the use of their work. If you notice any error or omission, please notify the publisher so that corrections can be incorporated into future editions of this work.

The information provided in this book hopes to inspire and inform. The author and publisher assume no responsibility for the effects, or lack thereof, obtained from the practices described in this book.

FOR MARY

'And I saw in the right hand of him who was seated on the throne a scroll written within and on the back, sealed with seven seals; and I saw a strong angel proclaiming with a loud voice......

Who is worthy to open the scroll and break its seals?'

Revelation 5:1

About the Author

Gary St. M. Nottingham first came across alchemy when he was fifteen through reading the popular early 1970's occult magazine *'Man, Myth & Magic'*

This encouraged him to find out further about the arte and to study Israel Regardie's 'The Philosopher's Stone'; this in turn led to the works of Hollandus, Paracelsus and eventually Junius. However, it was his involvement with a group of alchemical practitioners that opened many of the doors for him and much that he had learnt finally began to make sense.

Subsequently he has taught and written extensively on the alchemical arte, running several one-day workshops and weekends on practical laboratory alchemy.

His other areas of occult study are astrology, grimoires, and the Kabbalah, all of which are expressed as part of his alchemical work.

Table of Contents

About the Author 6
Introduction by Benjamin Turale 9

God is in All Things 15
Of the Body: its Material and Construct 23
The Magic of Numbers 29
As I Do Will… So Mote It Be 37
Of the Lords Who Wander 55
Of the Mansions of the Moon 96

Further reading 132

Index 133

```
ABRACADABRA
ABRACADABR
ABRACADAB
ABRACADA
ABRACAD
ABRACA
ABRAC
ABRA
ABR
AB
A
```

Introduction

The theoria and praxis Gary has outlined in this book first came to my attention at the 2018 Glastonbury Alchemy Conference, subsequently opening a whole new vista of practice for me. The talisman created there assisted me to attain a life-long goal, and it is this short story that I wish to share now in the hope that it inspires the reader, and shows them what is possible when we dare to undertake what is written in these pages.

The three-day conference event was originally conceived with the intention of giving attendees information and practice in techniques from two major streams of western occultism: magic and hermetic alchemy. Not having met Gary before the event he came highly recommended on the scene as being an adept practitioner in both disciplines, itself a rarity in the occult world. I asked Gary to put together a lecture which he duly delivered, choosing to speak on Basil Valentine's five considerations, as well as a 2-hour workshop intended to give attendees a memorable experience they could take away with them. His workshop did not disappoint. "The Arte of Talismanic Magic: Their Care, Construction and Enchantment" pointed attendees to the theoretical knowledge of astral forces that are required to make talismans effective. It also gave an overview of the traditional methods of theurgia which are so necessary to breathe life into the creation. In short, a lot of the information you are now holding in your hands. Gary put a lot of effort into the workshop, providing everyone with the necessary materials to create their own talisman on the spot. After this, attendees participated in a group ritual in which everyone had a chance to walk through the method from beginning to end, in order that they could both etch and animate their own solar brass talisman.

Gary and I had planned in advance to synchronise our conference work. I was creating a Roman chamomile tincture to demonstrate in my alchemy workshop, and we hit upon the idea to use his magical rite to consecrate not only the talismans, but also the tincture. With the ritual to be run on the Sunday of the conference, the herb was chosen, like the talisman, for its solar rulership. The tincture would also be finished at the conference and distributed to all participants, labelled with the same sigil that was on the brass talisman similarly consecrated. Thus participants would walk away with a "tincture of the sun", and a "talisman of the sun", which could be used separately (or in tandem for enhanced efficacy). It should be noted at this point that the metal associated with the sun is gold. Gold is perfection, representative of the alchemical *prima materia* taken to its highest state.

I have very fond memories of that ritual. So it was that without prior planning, barely minutes before the ritual started, the moon shifted into Leo – the astrological star sign associated with the Sun. Gary said "the Gods are with us" and you could feel a wave of excitement spread through the crowd. This itself was one of a long list of strange synchronicities that occurred around the event.

Synchronicity is certainly the force of magic in motion. I once attended a talk by the UK *Hermetic Order of the Golden Dawn*, where a senior adept said that "the magician walks hand in hand with synchronicity". For those of us in the know, synchronicity is proof that ritual magic works. I chose St. Dunstan as the patron saint of our conference, because he was the patron saint of alchemists in Emperor Rudolf II's court. The reason for this honour was that John Dee and Edward Kelley had used the Book of St. Dunstan as their instructional text to help them confect their Red Powder – their Philosopher's Stone, in which they demonstrated a transmutation of base metal to gold in front of Emperor Rudolf. To bring this historical arc full circle, the alchemy guild I represented at the conference traced its origins back to the Court of Emperor Rudolf II, and here I was co-ordinating this conference, in Glastonbury no less, where St. Dunstan was the Abbot over a thousand years ago. If you can possibly believe it, when I was choosing dates for the conference, I randomly selected with the co-ordinators of the Glastonbury Assembly Rooms three days to hire their space, one of which I found out much later was St. Dunstan's feast day! Other synchronicities stacked up the more I researched: Dee was baptised in the church of St. Dunstan in London. St. Dunstan's day in England is the day new gold is assayed. So there were dots being joined everywhere. In moments such as those, standing mere metres away from the Abbey in which St. Dunstan practised alchemy so long ago, with a small shrine set up at the rear of the hall to him, it was hard not to feel that everything was coming together. And with Dunstan's reputation as a conjuror when he was a young man, it seemed all the more apt.

The rite went off rather well, starting with banishing negative influences from the space. A circle of art was consecrated. It was then quite something to hear 50 people all invoking the sun in Latin at the same time. The ritual built up with sacred words spoken, solar incense burnt, the talismans consecrated by passing them through the smoke, finally culminating in everyone visualising the solar king seated on his throne in the herbal tincture upon the altar. It highlighted for me the power to use these methods not just on talismans, but to further charge alchemical preparations themselves with stellar energy/archetypes, to be consumed at a time when needed. My recommendation to any readers with knowledge of the alchemical spagyric arts is to time the crystallisation of philosophic salts at the desired moment of astral influence. This could also be the time when a tincture or other preparation is consecrated magically. The time a substance becomes fixed (as the salts) is when matter goes from being merely a liquid (and full of all the different astral influences) to become fixed in an astrological moment in time, just as a human does at birth.

At the conclusion of the conference I had made many new friendships. The event was a success on many levels, yet the doing of it was reward enough itself. However what was really setting me aflame at that time in my alchemical practice was my pursuit of learning how to make a true alchemical oil (soul) of gold. This is a preparation which contains no actual gold metal in it (i.e. not a colloidal), but where the colour, the medicinal profile of the gold is present, ready to be drunk and embodied. This is one of the many secrets of alchemy – as Stephanos of

Alexandria said "alchemy is the ability to separate souls from bodies". So it was that during the ritual at the conference this wish was sitting in the back of my mind.

Many many moons and another story arc later, when I finally successfully created the gold oil (and immediately afterwards experienced a bolt of lightning strike mere feet from my window), I decided to consecrate the gold oil to the solar energy using the methods Gary taught me. I performed the rite when the moon was in Leo. At its conclusion, I drew the solar kamea on the reagent bottle in golden ink. Some time later I looked at the bottle, but all did not seem right for such a fine product to be painted with such a crude marker. It needed something more splendid. I was struck in this moment to remember the talisman created at the conference so long ago. I found the talisman, and when I tied it to the bottle, a wave of realisation came over me. The journey was complete, the wish fulfilled and a life dream coagulated from the volatile light of imagination into the fixed light of reality. As I sat there reflecting on the series of events that led me to the ritual in 2018, I began to realize something else. The magic circle of arte we draw on the ground exists as a microcosm of the greater world (macrocosm). In it, ritual time is circular and therefore does not exist only in one direction - rituals work backwards in time, as our wishes carry us forward inexorably to our casting of them.

The talisman I created using the very methods Gary has outlined in this book helped guide me, inevitably, to both my inner and outer gold. It took me on a journey to arrive at my own microcosmic sun.

Fate led me to these methods just as you have now been led to them. My wish is that this masterwork may serve you as it has served me.

What treasures await in your future? What golden dream does the universe weave into the yearning of your heart's true wish?

Journey well.

Benjamin Turale | Director, the Temple of Mercury.
www.thetempleofmercury.com

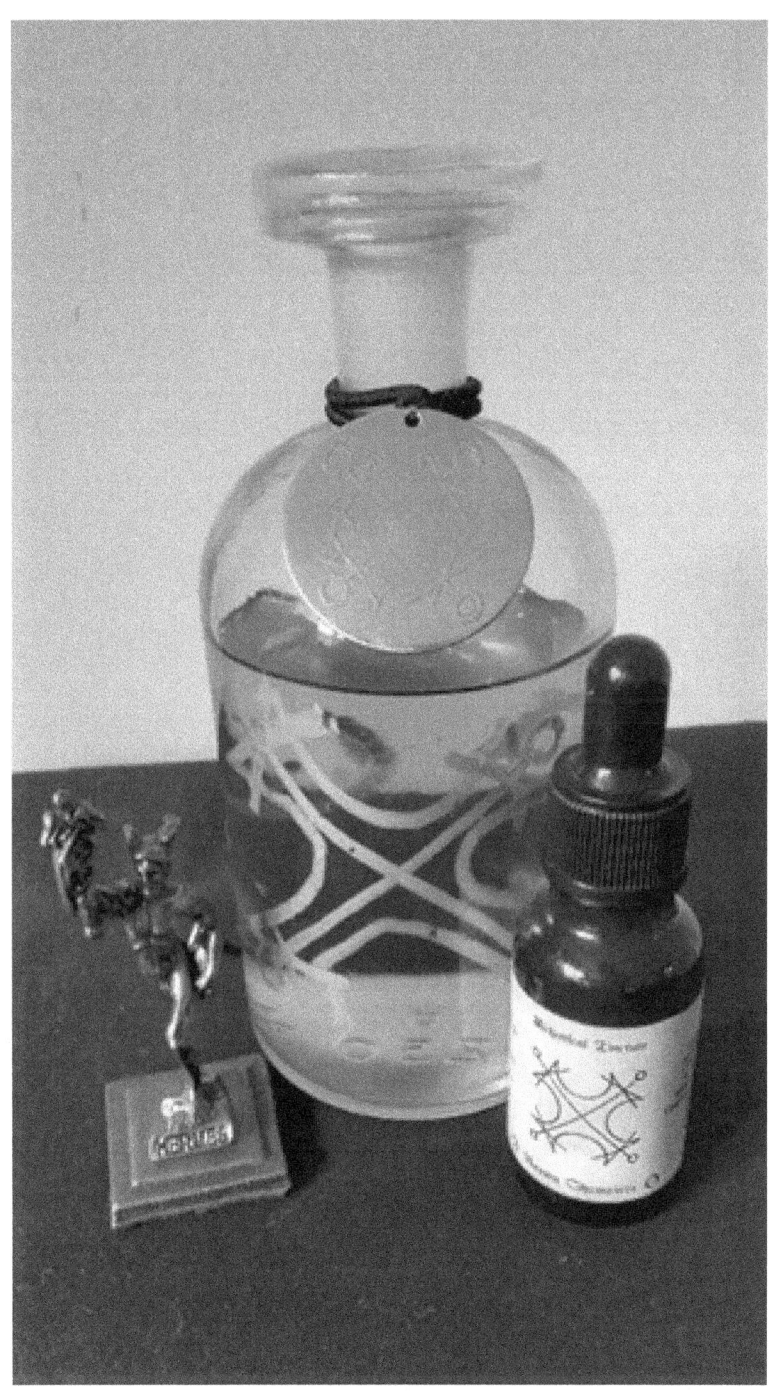

Tincture of Chamomile, Oil of Gold and the Solar Talisman

CHAPTER ONE
God is in All Things

God is in all things, as their root and the source of their being. There is nothing that has not a source, but the source itself springs from nothing but itself, if it is the source of all else.

Corpus Hermeticum Book IV

Writing in her noted work *Psychic Self-Defence* Dion Fortune made the following observation that is of supreme relevance to our work:

'We live in the midst of invisible forces whose effects alone we perceive. We move among invisible forms whose actions we very often do not perceive at all… although we may be profoundly affected by them.'

It is these energies that flow throughout creation, and which we are part of, that we endeavour to connect with by our will and magical prowess, as we seek to challenge our destiny, and indeed those of others too. Subsequently, by the use of our magic, we seek to challenge our fate. For we are no longer passive, and the recipients of the favours of the Gods… We seek to challenge them and with their own potencies too, as we become players in the Great Game of Life. It is the powers that are represented by the four elements and the seven planets of the ancient world, the 'Lords Who Wander', which this work primarily calls upon, as ingress into their realms and access to the powers thereof are made manifest.

Talismanic magic has been an important part of the Western Magical Corpus, and this work explores their construction and consecration, thus allowing a little-used magical practice to become part of our magical armoury. The sorcerer creates the outer form of the talisman which they then endeavour, by their magical will, to ensoul with higher energies, or sometimes with those of a demonic nature should that be deemed suitable to the working. Talismans become like batteries of magical power, pulsating their energies throughout the planes and the everyday world. They need to be cared for; some will need to be re-charged regularly, particularly when they are working on a long term and difficult problem. Whilst planetary or elemental energies can be used to empower them, they can also be consecrated by having a particular spirit bound to the seal, which is released when the magic has come to fruition. The consecration of them can be complex, but it can be simple too. This work will explore the various means to empower your talismans for all manner of outcomes, and it will draw no moral judgements upon your endeavours. I say this as there have been times in my life when I have not been quite sure whether it's me working the magic or the magic working me. Is it fate prodding you to perform your working or are the Gods using you to open the door to a particular energy manifesting? Or is it just you doing what you want? One needs to be circumspect as it can be tempting to try and unleash all manner of outcomes, and when they manifest they may not always be what you wanted... So thought is needed, as magic will often take the shortest route to manifestation.

Our talismans can be created from a variety of materials, stone, paper and metal being the favourites. Although writing in the 9th century, the work *De Imaginibus* of Thabit Ibn Qurra makes it quite clear that the material which is used to form the talisman is not important..... this goes against much of the received talismanic wisdom from the Middle Ages until today, but De Imaginibus makes it quite clear that the most important part of creating talismans is getting the astral timing right. Hence the importance of astrology. Indeed, reading this important work on our arte it becomes quite clear that talismanic work is dependent upon the stars rather than the operator. There has been more than one occasion when someone has said to me how they had gone to great lengths and indeed expense over a particular planetary rite and it failed miserably. I then ask about the astrology of the working. Of course, such things as waxing moons, planetary hours and days will have all been taken into consideration, as one would expect. 'But what of the planet itself.' I ask. 'Is it retrograde?' (meaning, does it seem from the earth to be going backwards?) 'Is it in a sign where it is weak or strong? Perhaps it's badly aspected by a malefic planet?' (Mars or Saturn) A malefic aspect would be when the planet in question receives a square, which is when the two planets are 90° apart. Or it receives an opposition, that is when the planet is receiving another planet 180° from it. A conjunction is when two planets are occupying the same degree of the zodiac, and this can be good unless the planet that is conjuncting the one you are working with is Saturn or Mars. Both will destroy the work so it will be best to wait until the aspect has passed, which will happen when the planets are more than two degrees apart. Another consideration will be the moon: does she assist or hinder? Is she making a good aspect? Invariably, on a forensic examination of the working, it often becomes quite clear that the planet is unable to help owing to a detrimental placement or aspect, and it is such considerations as these which will help or hinder the success of your magical will to manifest accordingly.

Writing in his work *Traite Elementaire de Magie Pratique* (Elementary Treatise on Practical Magic), Papus tells us that the talisman is the material sign of the joining of the will of the Magister with an astral influence. He also explains that one must create and consecrate the talisman when the moon makes a good aspect to the planet that you are working with, and as the moon travels around the zodiac in a month there will be several times when the moon will favour the work through being domiciled in one of the planets' houses, or when she conjuncts, sextiles or trines the planet in question. He tells us that were we to create our talisman simply by using planetary days and hours then we cannot expect its influence to last more than a month. However, if the talisman is created when the moon is domiciled in the planetary house, for example if creating a Venusian talisman (always popular) then it would be better for the moon to be in one of Venus's houses such as Libra or Taurus. (Avoid this if the moon is 15° or more in Libra as she will then be part of the Via Combusta and she will not be happy domiciled in this part of Libra). I would prefer Taurus as the moon is strong in this sign and this would greatly favour such a working. If we applied this rule then we could expect the talisman's power to last for a year or even more, particularly if the Sun is also making a favourable aspect to the planet at the time of working.

Thus, on such a day, and I would ignore whether it is the planet's day or not, that if you work within the planetary hour. This will suffice and your work will then be more likely to be successful. However, if circumstances are such and perhaps you cannot wait until such a favourable time, then consider whether the planet or the moon has any dignity by term or by face. Each sign of the zodiac can be divided into three groups of 10° giving 36 groups of 10° over the whole of the twelve signs of the zodiac. These are known as decans and each group will have a planetary association.

The first 10° of each sign will be ruled by the planet of that sign. Therefore, the first 10° of Aries, for example, will be ruled by Mars, the governing planet of that sign. As it is a fire sign we consider the next fire sign which is Leo and therefore the second group of 10° of Aries will answer to the Sun as the ruler of Leo. Finally the last 10° of Aries comes under the remaining fire sign Sagittarius, thus Jupiter as its ruling planet will dominate the last 10° of Aries.

I offer this for consideration because we can also work when the moon is in the decan or 'Face' as the ancients called it, of the planet in question. With this formula the other houses can quite easily be considered. However, waiting for a planet can be slow: the moon will move as much as 13° in a day whilst the more slowly-moving planets, like Saturn, will take as much as thirty months to move through a sign.

If for example you are working with Venus and she were to be domiciled in Aries, here she is weak and unable to do much. As she moves about a degree a day wait until she moves into her own sign of Taurus, particularly the first 10°, where she will be at her strongest, potent and able to assist you…. more so when the moon too is domiciled in her sign or makes a good aspect to her.

One final consideration is the Head and Tail of the Dragon. These are also known as the north node, the Head, and the south node, the Tail. Both refer to the moon and the angle made as she crosses the ecliptic. Although they were used in medieval magic, they have become less significant in today's magical practice and often ignored, something I feel to the magical worker's detriment. The Head of the Dragon, symbolised by ☊, is considered to be of the nature of Jupiter and Venus and is beneficial. Whilst the Tail of the Dragon whose symbol is such ☋ is of the nature of Saturn and Mars and is therefore detrimental to the success of your working, and must be avoided. Do not work when the tail aspects the planet you are endeavouring to work with, nor when the moon herself is conjunct, square or in opposition to the Tail of the Dragon. Any workings that are performed when the moon is in the 'Burning Way' known as the Via Combusta, which is between 15° Libra to 15° Scorpio, are unlikely to promote a successful outcome, as this is a negative place for the moon to dwell, unless she is at 23° Libra where the beneficial star Spica is domiciled, here she would be safe.

Indeed, some practitioners would consider that if any planet is traversing through this area of the zodiac then it is in a bad way and cannot help you.

One final astrological consideration is the Sun. Traditionally the Sun is a benevolent planet, which it is. However, owing to the might of its power, it can sometimes 'overpower' another planet. In traditional astrology there are definite rules regarding this and I feel they are also relevant for the success of talismanic magic. Therefore, we must consider Doretheus who taught that the Sun's rays are so powerful they can obscure or burn any planet that gets too close to it. In this situation the Sun will dominate the planet and it will not be free to act for you. The degrees to consider for the planet which you are working with are 17° to 8° away from the Sun and whether it is going to the Sun's position or leaving it. Here the planet is 'Under the Sunbeams,' and is weakened. If the planet is, however, between 8° and 0.5° then it is considered to be combust and will be greatly weakened by the dominance of the Sun's power and therefore not free to act for you. But when it is exactly conjunct the Sun between 0.5° - 0°, here it is cazimi, or in the heart of the Sun and very strong as the power of the Sun will enhance the potency of the planet. Therefore it can be seen quite clearly that when the astral tides are flowing in your favour success is more likely to be forthcoming. (see the Table of essential dignity and debilities at the end of this chapter)

A talisman can have a persistent effect and be extremely useful in a variety of operations. Once it is created, and with due practice and attention, the talisman will over time build a momentum that will be working both day and night as the energies manifest your desire in the material world or at other levels of being as you deem relevant. This is a good means of magical expression if you want a long-term effect to occur, although it is not limited to such results alone.

However, as you have brought it into birth, the talisman will be connected to your psyche. It then becomes your magical child, and as such will have a psychic connection with you. This must be severed as the talisman can, under certain circumstances become a drain upon your own etheric energies and feed off you instead of the wider etheric energies of creation. This is why you cannot simply abandon a talisman and forget about it. When it has run its course and its work is done, it must then be deconsecrated and any energies attached to it need to be released back to the cosmos. A talisman can be rendered ineffective by the magician even if it is not in their keeping and is elsewhere.

By the use of the holy names of the Kabbalah and the various levels of existence the talisman will be connected to the source of all by the use of the God Name most relevant to the operation. The imagery and design will correspond to the energies which become ensouled by the work. Thus, the talisman becomes the centre of certain ideas and imagery, such as colour, form and design, which will resonate with the concepts invoked. These will then become energised during the consecration ritual, as the talisman is ensouled by the descending etheric force which responds to the patterns created on the astral levels. This is the critical point because if these are inadequately formed then the descending forces will not ensoul the talisman sufficiently for your will to manifest.

Looking at grimoire material and other texts from the middle ages, it is quite clear in most of them that the empowering words and phrases are often drawn from the Christian mythos, as Jesus Christ, or his mother and the saints are invoked to aid the conjuror. There is, in my view, nothing wrong in this as these works use imagery and names which the conjuror of the time would have been familiar with and would have had some emotional connection to. Which seems to me to have been some of the driving force of the working. With this in mind Kabbalistic imagery and words will work for you, particularly if you have some resonance with them as they will then provide that emotional link which is needed for them to become active in your magic. To do this you will find it useful to have used the methods of meditation, pathwork and ritual to create that link in your psyche necessary for them to become alive.

Therefore, having created your talisman and consecrated it, it has now become a physical expression of a nonphysical force that is active in bringing your will to birth…
'As I do will… So Mote It Be!'

Sign	♈	♉	♊	♋	♌	♍	♎	♏	♐	♑	♒	♓
Ruler	♂	♀	☿	☽	☉	☿	♀	♂	♃	♄	♄	♃
Exaltation	☉	☽	☊	♃		☿	♄		☋	♂		♀
Decan 0-10	♈	♀	☿	☽	☉	☿	♀	♂	♃	♄	♄	♃
10-20	☉	☿	♀	♂	♃	♄	♄	♃	♂	♀	☿	☽
20-30	♃	♄	♄	♃	♂	♀	☿	☽		☿	♀	♂
Detriment	♀	♂	♄	♄	♄	♃	♂	♀	☿	☽	☉	☿
Fall	♄		☋	♂		♀	☉	☽	☊	♃		☿

Essential Planetary Dignities and Debilities
After Master Lilly

CHAPTER TWO
Of the Body: its Material and Construct

In 1801 Francis Barrett, compiler of the magical text, *'The Magus'* made it quite clear that:

> *'The virtue of consecrations chiefly consists in two things. The power of the person consecrating and the virtue of the prayer by which the consecrations are made.'*

He also tells us:

> *'For in the person consecrating, there is required firmness, constancy and holiness of life; and that the consecrator himself shall, with a firm and indubitable faith, believe the virtue, power and effect thereof. Then in the prayer by which the consecration is made it derives its virtue either from divine inspiration, or else by composing it from sundry places in the holy Scriptures, in the commemoration of some of the wonderful miracles of God, effects, promises, sacraments and sacramental things, of which we have abundance in holy writ.*
>
> *There must likewise be used the invocation of divine names, that are significative of the work in hand.; likewise a sanctifying and expiation which is wrought by sprinkling with holy water, unctions with holy oil, and odoriferous suffumigations. Therefore, in every consecration there is generally used a benediction and consecration of water, earth, oil, fire and suffumigations etc. with consecrated wax-lights or lamps burning; for without lights no consecration is duly performed. You must therefore particularly observe this, that when anything (which we call profane) is to be used, in which there is any defilement or pollution, it must, first of all, be purified by an Exorcism composed solely for that purpose, which ought to proceed*

> *the consecration; which things being so made pure are most apt to receive the influences of the divine virtue."*

Furthermore, he tells us that....

> *'We must also observe that at the end of any consecration after the prayer is rightly performed, as we have mentioned, the operator ought to bless the thing consecrated, by breathing out some sentence with divine virtue and power of the present consecration, with a commemoration of his virtue and authority, that so it may be the more duly performed, and with an earnest and attentive mind.'*

Bearing in mind Barrett's observations and good advice, we may attend upon our arte accordingly.

Whilst the previously mentioned work *De Imaginibus* makes it quite clear that the material of the body of the talisman is of little consideration, the talismanic arte has always been quite clear in its instructions regarding what colours and materials are to be used. The Greater Key of Solomon, for example, clearly states that the use of colour, consecrated pens and paper are to be used to great advantage. Seals which are engraved upon gemstones or rings are also worthy of note, but I also want to explore the arte of etching talismanic designs upon metal, something which is easy to do and very effective, and yet it is little known.

Solomon advises us to keep inks, paper and pens separate and consecrated for talismanic construction. He is clear that we must consecrate these items prior to any work and this will be our first act. Although he suggests that we use the skin of a sacrificed animal and create our own parchment from it, this is something which we will not do, particularly as he makes it quite clear that we can also use parchment, although I would consider a decent quality paper as an alternative, particularly if it has been 'dressed' with a fluid condenser as (see Franz Bardon's *Initiation into Hermetics*) or added to any inks or paints that are being used as these are deemed to act like psychic batteries and will enhance the ability of the parchment or paper to hold the magical charge.

Therefore, on a waxing moon, when she is domiciled in the sign of Gemini or Virgo, take, in the hour of Mercury, the material that you will use for your future talismans and consecrate accordingly:

> Facing east perform the Q/C:
>
> Say:

'Blessed art thou Lord of Creation for thy glory flows out never ending.'

> Sprinkle with consecrated water saying:

'Let all malignancy and hindrance be cast forth hencefrom so that all good may enter herein.'

> Cense with incense saying:

*'In the Holy Names Agla Yod He Vau He Iah Emanuel
Bless and preserve this parchment/paper
so that no phantasm may enter therein.'*

> Trace an equal-armed cross over the material and say:

*'Be ye present to aid me
and may my operation be accomplished through you:*

*Zazaii Zalmaii Dalmaii Adonai Anaphaxeton Cedrion Cripon Prion Anaireton Elion Octinomon Zevanion Alzaion Zideon Agla On Yod He Vau He Artor Dinotor Holy Angels of God be present and infuse virtue into this parchment/paper so that it may obtain such power through you that all Names and Characters thereon written may receive due power and that all deceit and hindrance may depart therefrom through God the Lord merciful and gracious.
Who liveth and reigneth through all Ages.
Amen.'*

If you are using a gemstone for the body of your talisman or a metal disc which you intend to engrave, it too would benefit from this rite and prepare it for future consecration.

The pens and inks will also need to be consecrated. If you are using a pen which has the ink inside (which is normally the case), as opposed to a dip pen which traditionally would have been used, this is no problem as the following consecration will suffice for both types.

> Sprinkle the pen with holy water and say:

*'Adrai Hahlii Tamii Tilonas Athamas Zianor Adonai
Banish from this pen all deceit and error*

So that it may be of virtue and efficacy to write all that I desire.'

Trace an equal-armed cross in the air over the ink or the pen. However, if the ink is in the pen say also:

'I exorcise thee O creature of ink by Anaireton by Simulator and by the name Adonai and by the name of him through whom all things were made that thou be unto me an aid and succour in all things which I wish to perform by thy aid.'

Any engraving tool, which will then be the magical burin, may be consecrated by the use of the wording for the pen by changing the terms accordingly.

Concerning the etching of metals, this is a simple task and one that has much to commend it as it can produce a longer-lasting talisman of pleasing design.

The best metals for etching in my experience are brass, copper and iron. For this we will be using ferric chloride which is cheap and easy to acquire via the internet. Gold is not ,as far as I'm aware, suitable for etching. Silver can be etched but it is a much more complex operation - although there are plenty of examples to be seen via YouTube, should you wish to explore this approach. If you plan to engrave the metal it is best to draw the design with a fine-tipped permanent marker pen and then go over the design with your etching tool. You will then be less likely to make a mistake.

Therefore, to etch your talisman you will need ferric chloride, a dish in which to hold the talisman whilst it is being etched, and a permanent marker pen – I would suggest obtaining pens whose nibs are of a variety of thicknesses for fine work. You will need tape to cover the back, unless you are etching that as well. Also useful will be ruler and stencils with different size circles, triangles and squares. Plus, some very fine wire wool for polishing.

Having invoked a blessing on our work and in the planetary hour we draw the talisman design upon our metal disk. It is then placed in the container and covered with ferric chloride to the depth of 30mm thereabouts. The seal is left in the etching fluid for 50-60 minutes after which it is taken out. It will be marked clearly by the pen lines, which after the seal having been washed and polished with the wire wool will be removed, with the talisman becoming clean, shiny and ready for the charging by your magical will.

TOOLS NEEDED: BRASS DISC, DISH, PERMANENT MARKER PEN, FERRIC CHLORIDE, FINE WIRE WOOL.

THE DESIGN FOR ETCHING

In the etching fluid

Retrieved talisman after 50-60 minutes and the end result after polishing the seal with fine grade wire wool.

CHAPTER THREE
The Magic of Numbers

Numbers are a magical thing and are considered by some to be the means by which the universe has been created. The sacredness of number has been appreciated by various cultures and has found expression in the construction of a variety of sacred buildings. In our magical arte we can use number to create personalized talismans whereby the individual can have their name - which of course is an expression of themselves - linked to a particular current.

By changing the letters of one's name into numbers and then tracing the numbers on to a planetary square we will have a design to etch or draw as our talisman. The planetary square will give the current to which we are endeavouring to link and call into our lives. A suitable biblical verse is sometimes inscribed on the back of the talisman to re-enforce the concepts which it represents and is verbally repeated in the consecration rite. Around the seal itself the God Name that governs the planet can be inscribed or a simple sentence encapsulating your intent, which can be drawn in a magical alphabet. The use of magical alphabets will be far more potent if you know the letters and can draw them without consulting a script. For by knowing them, they have become part of your own psyche which will help to empower them.

THEBAN SCRIPT

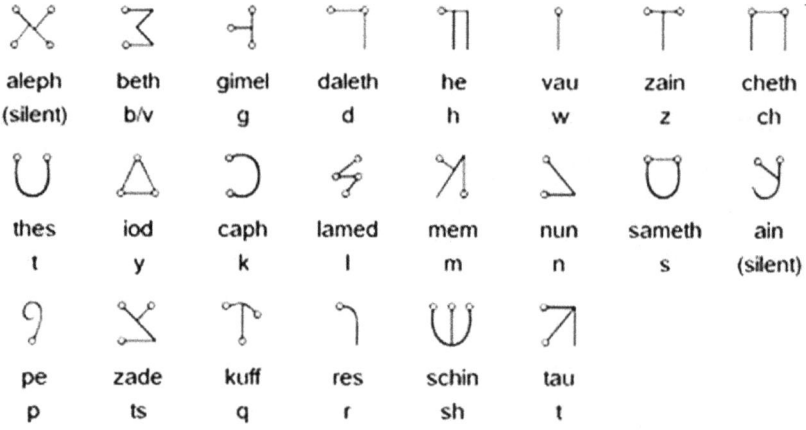

CELESTIAL SCRIPT: BASED ON THE TWENTY-TWO HEBREW LETTERS

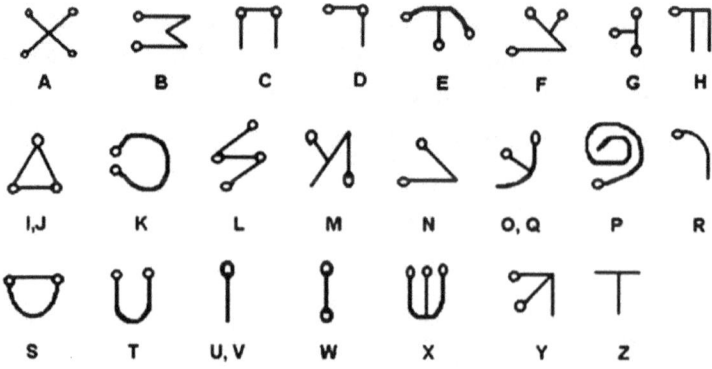

ANGLICIZED VERSION OF ABOVE

1	2	3	4	5	6	7	8	9
A	B	C	D	E	F	G	H	I
J	K	L	M	N	O	P	Q	R
S	T	U	V	W	X	Y	Z	

THE ALPHABET OF NUMBERS

PLANETARY KAMEA

These are various combinations of number upon a grid system which represents the planet to which they are attributed. Each square will contain the number which is associated Kabbalistically with each planet. For example the Saturn kamea consists of a grid on 3x3 squares, 3 being the number of Saturn. The Jupiter kamea will be made of 4x4 squares, the number of Jupiter.

The other kamea will follow this pattern.

Saturn

4	9	2
3	5	7
8	1	6

Jupiter

4	14	15	1
9	7	6	12
5	11	10	8
16	2	3	13

Mars

11	24	7	20	3
4	12	25	8	16
17	5	13	21	9
10	18	1	14	22
23	6	19	2	15

Sun

6	32	33	34	35	1
25	11	27	28	8	30
19	20	16	15	23	24
13	14	22	21	17	18
7	29	9	10	26	12
36	2	3	4	5	31

Venus

22	47	16	41	10	35	4
5	23	48	17	42	11	29
30	6	24	49	18	36	12
13	31	7	25	43	19	37
38	14	32	1	26	44	20
21	39	8	33	2	27	45
46	15	40	9	34	3	28

Mercury

8	58	59	5	4	62	63	1
49	15	14	52	53	11	10	56
41	23	22	44	45	19	18	48
32	34	35	29	28	38	39	25
40	26	27	37	36	30	31	33
17	47	46	20	21	43	42	24
9	55	54	12	13	51	50	16
64	2	3	61	60	6	7	57

Luna

37	78	29	70	21	62	13	54	5
6	38	79	30	71	22	63	14	46
47	7	39	80	31	72	23	55	15
16	48	8	40	81	32	64	24	56
57	17	49	9	41	73	33	65	25
26	58	18	50	1	42	74	34	66
67	27	59	10	51	2	43	75	35
36	68	19	60	11	52	3	44	76
77	28	69	20	61	12	53	4	45

Therefore, to make a talisman which links you to a particular planetary current we chose our astrological timing and trace our name on the relevant planetary kamea accordingly. Use the name that you identify with. So, for example, if we wish to draw the solar current into our lives and we use the name David , we consider the numbers on our Alphabet of Numbers and write the name in numbers thus:

D=4   A=1   V=4   I=9   D=4

These are now traced out over the Sun kamea giving the following sigil which can now be etched or drawn as we see fit to create the talisman of the name.

THE SIGIL OF THE NAME DAVID TRACED OVER THE SUN KAMEA

The double circle will have the names of the Sun written around the edge.

However, we can also use this concept for such works as binding or blasting someone or something. To bind, trace the name of your foe on the Saturn kamea or Mars should you deem it relevant and you wish to apply a more 'muscular approach.'

Here we have the name Boris traced upon the Saturn kamea and the sigil placed within the double circle around which would be written the names that govern the energies of Saturn.

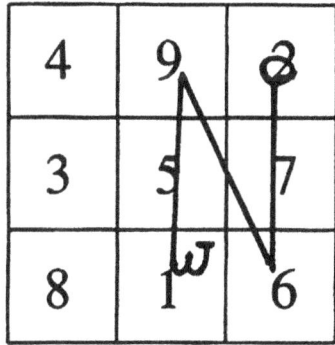

Boris: B=2   O=6   R=9   I=9   S=1.

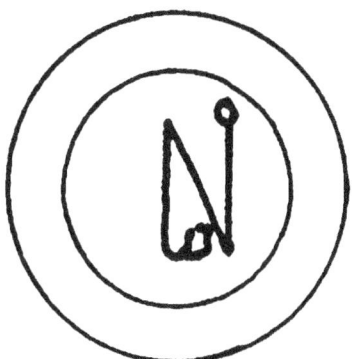

THE NAME BORIS AS A SIGIL OF SATURN

The sigil starts with a circle on the line and ends with a line across at the finish.

Here the Boris sigil, when consecrated, could be buried preferably in a churchyard to hold the individual, or it could even be placed in the freezer. Which from past experience I know will work well, as I was asked by someone, many years ago, to bind their in-laws from popping around all the time. I used a variant of this spell and placed the seal in the freezer, which I am pleased to say 'worked like a charm.' As one would expect.

However, I experienced a power cut one day and the freezer thawed out and the individual again became plagued with unwanted relatives. But such is life.

CHAPTER FOUR
As I Do Will... So Mote It Be

This chapter presents a medley of several talismans and their detailed construction according to our arte which the practitioner will find useful. They all have a consecration rite given and their astrological timing is also considered. They may be made in metal or drawn upon parchment or paper as already considered, although metal will make them more lasting. By constructing our talisman, we are creating a portal for the energies which they represent to manifest in the everyday world, however the consecration and charging of them may need to be performed more than once, as the energies will dissipate in time and with some situations more than one charging may be necessary for the talisman to achieve your will. With a competent ritual there will be an outpouring of emotion which will be directed at the object of one's desire. As this happens, we are pouring out a subtle but nonetheless potent form of force and this will help to ensoul the thought-form which the ritual is building up. As the mental picture of one's desire becomes ensouled by this force it starts to live upon the astral levels and is a real substance at its own level. By creating the physical body in the everyday world, we can use this for the energies to manifest in our world.

While they can be consecrated by complex rites and rituals this is not always necessary or needed. Some time ago I was given some ritual material from a pre-war French occult group that used a simple method of talismanic consecration. Basically, the idea was that the talisman is wrapped in silk, which is a psychic insulator, and is unwrapped during the planetary hour and left to 'soak up' the planetary energies. Then it is covered up and put away until the planetary hour should come around again, whereby the steps previously performed are repeated. This will in time charge the talisman with the planetary energies.

However, while this simple approach will work, I would suggest the following additional practices. Firstly, do not forget the astrology of the working and let the planet that rules the work be unhindered, remember it must have no bad aspects from Mars or Saturn such as conjunctions, squares or oppositions. Make sure it is not in a house where it is weak and cannot work for you adequately.

By lighting a candle of the planet's colour we are marking the presence of the energies with which we are endeavouring to work with. Let the talisman be blessed and dedicated and held in the rising incense fumes whilst you say the invocation.

Then leave it to 'soak up' the astral vibe of the planetary hour, and when it is finished simply wrap it in a clean piece of silk. This simple rite can be repeated at the next planetary hour which will further help to charge it.

THE ABRA CADABRA CHARM

Writing in the *Straggling Astrologer*, an occult magazine of 1824, Robert Cross-Smith (better known as Raphael) published the following talisman which he claimed was in the keeping of a late Georgian occult group based in the UK and known to its members as the Mercurii.... This talisman became popular among the conjurors of mid-Wales and along the border with England, with several original charms still in existence. Working with this charm will connect you with their current. The Abra Cadabra charm, Raphael tells us, is used to heal but by a change of intent it can also be used to banish or if reversed, even to attract, as will be explained.

ABRACADABRA
ABRACADABR
ABRACADAB
ABRACADA
ABRACAD
ABRACA
ABRAC
ABRA
ABR
AB
A

The letters of this charm are to be written on virgin paper although you could engrave it on brass. The charm is to be worn by the individual for whom it is intended for one month as the moon travels through all the signs of the zodiac.

Raphael suggests that the charm is to be created when the moon is full and in the signs of Sagittarius or Pisces. Which suggests that it is Jupiterian by nature, as both these signs are governed by the great benefic. However, to follow this pattern would mean that the sun will be in Gemini or Virgo. If you cannot wait until then I would suggest that you could work with this charm when the moon is waxing (to gain health) and the moon is domiciled in either Sagittarius or Pisces and not necessarily full. This is quite a simple talisman and Raphael tells us to repeat the following oration when it is made and in difficult cases to recite it every day until cured. To do this I would suggest that you hold it, if possible, in a Jupiterian incense whilst reciting the following invocation:

'O sweet Lord Jesus Christ + the true God, who didst descend from the kingdom of thy Almighty Father, being sent to wash away our sins.

To release those who were in prison and afflicted, to console the sorrowful and the needy, to absolve and liberate me, thy servant, from my affliction and tribulation in which I am placed. So, O, Omnipotent Father thou didst receive us again by his expiation into that paradise by thy blood. O Jesu + obtained and didst make us equal among angels and men. Thou O Lord Jesus Christ + wert worthy to stand between me and mine enemies and to establish my peace and to show thy grace upon me and to pour out thy mercy. And thou O Lord Jesus + extend thine arm towards me and deliver me from my affliction even as thou didst deliver Abraham from the Chaldean and his son Isaac from the sacrifice and Jacob from the hand of his brethren. Noah from the deluge and even as thou didst deliver thy servant Lot, thy servants Moses and Aaron, and thy people Israel from the hands of Pharaoh and out of the land of Egypt. David from the hands of Saul, and the giant Goliath; or as thou delivered Susannah from her accusers. Judith from the hands of Holofernes, Daniel from the den of lions, the three youths from the fiery furnace. Jonah from the whale's belly, or as thou deliverest the son of Cannanae who was tormented by the devil, even as thou deliverest Adam from hell by thy most precious blood, and Peter and Paul from chains. So O most sweet Lord Jesus + son of the Living God preserve me thy servant from my affliction and mine enemies and be my assistant and my blessing by thy holy incarnation by thy fasting and thirst by thy labours and affliction by thy stripes by thy thorny crown by thy drink of gall and vinegar by thy most cruel death by the words which thou spakest upon the cross by thy descent into hell by the consolation of thy disciples by thy wonderful ascension by the appearance of the Holy Spirit by the day of judgement, by thy great gifts and by thy holy names ADONAY + ELOYM+ HELOYM+ YACY+ZAZAEL+ PALIEL+ SADAY+ YZOE+ YARAS+ CAELPHI+ SADAY+ and by the thy ineffable name YHVH JEHOVAH+ By all these holy, omnipotent and all-powerful names of singular efficacy and extraordinary power, which the elements obey and at which the devils tremble: O most gracious Jesu + grant, I beseech thee, that this holy charm which I now wear about my person may be the means of healing my lamentable sickness so shall the praise thereof be ascribed O Lord to thee alone and thou alone shalt have all the glory. Amen.'

To work this charm at a distance for another person, the individual must scrape off a line of the charm every day with a new knife. The knife can be used on the rest of the charm - it doesn't need a new knife for every line scraped off. As you are doing so say:

'So as I destroy the letter of this charm ABRACADABRA so by virtue of the sacred name may all grief and dolor depart from XYZ
In the name of the Father and of the Son and of the Holy Ghost.
In the name of the Father I destroy this disease.
In the name of the Son I destroy this disease

and in the name of the Holy Spirit I destroy this disease. Amen.'

While Raphael tells us that the charm came from the Mercurii who in turn claimed that it was from the friar Robert Bacon, actually the charm originated in the Mediterranean world and was brought into this country [the United Kingdom] in the 2nd century by Roman physicians without the Christian adaptions.

With this format in mind, let us consider how we can change the intent of the charm for other purposes. In the case of binding or banishing let the moon be domiciled in a Saturnine house, or best conjunct Saturn, and let the working take place in the Saturnine hour. Without making the working too complex we can stay with the simple formula outlined above and use the oration given, but simply change the wording where relevant so that it will banish or bind accordingly. For example, towards the end it says:

> *'I beseech thee that this holy charm which I wear about my person may be the means of healing my lamentable sickness etc etc....'*

We could change this so that it reads...

> *'I beseech thee that this holy charm may bind or banish XYZ.'*

Then in the Saturn hour of each day following take your new knife as required and scrape out a line starting from the top as we want the charm to get smaller as we are banishing someone or something and as you do so say the following:

> *'As I destroy the letters of this charm ABRACADBRA*
> *So by the virtue of the sacred name may XYZ*
> *be bound or banished (change as needed)*
> *In the name of the Father I banish/bind XYZ*
> *In the name of the Son I banish/bind XYZ*
> *In the name of the Holy Ghost I banish/bind XYZ*
> *So that they may never......(state intent)*
> *So Mote It Be!*

Whilst we have been considering this talisman for banishing or binding someone or something, we could reverse it and draw someone or something towards us.

To do this take your clean piece of paper and a new pen, and write your name at the top, with your desire at the bottom, whether it be a person, a situation, money, a home, or a job etc. If you want someone in your life or friendship in general then you will need to work when the moon favours Venus, as we have already considered earlier, and also work in the Venusian hour. Using green ink, write the letter A above your written-down desire saying the following from the Song of Solomon:

'O that you would kiss me with the kisses of your mouth
For your love is better than wine
Your anointing oils are fragrant
Your name is oil poured out therefore the maidens love you
Draw me after you let us make haste
The king has brought me into his chambers we will exult and rejoice in you
We will extol your love more than wine rightly do they love you.'

Then say:

'In the name of the Father…..(state intent)
In the name of the Son…..(state intent)
And in power of the Holy Ghost….(state intent)'

The next day in the hour of Venus write the two letters AB above the letter A previously written and repeat the lines from the Song of Solomon with the above invocation.

On the third day, again in the hour of Venus, write above the letters AB… ABR and repeat the wording above. This is repeated the next day, following this format until on the eleventh day you reach the full name ABRACADABRA. Put the paper charm away until your will comes to pass.

For other works such as money, position, property, or the favour of those who are above you, work in the hour of Jupiter when he is favoured by the moon.

In blue ink write your name at the top of a clean piece of paper and that which you want to come to pass at the bottom.

Saying the following lines from the 23rd psalm:

The Lord is my Shepherd and I shall not want
He maketh me lie down in green pasture
He leadeth me beside still waters

And he restoreth my soul.'

Then repeat the formula that we used earlier, that is, on day one, write down the letter A and read from Psalm 23 again and state your intent, then recite the following invocation:

*'In the Name of the Father…(state intent)
In the Name of the Son…(state intent)
And by the power of the Holy Ghost….(state intent)'*

Next day in the Jupiter hour repeat the working, but write the letters AB above the letter A done previously. Follow this formula until you reach the ABRACADABRA on the eleventh day. Then put the charm away until your will manifests.

THE LLANYBLODWELL CHARM

The following talisman will help to protect you from all enemies and their wiles.

I first came across this talisman in the archives of the public library at Shrewsbury (UK), where it was shown without the inscription around the outer rim. With the remark that it was a charm which had been used by a farmer at Llanyblodwell (on the Welsh border) during the 19th century.

Further research led me to material by Robert Cross-Smith who had published it during the 1820's in the *Straggling Astrologer* with instructions for its creation. He tells us that the talisman comes under the domain of Jupiter and the Sun and that it should be created from tin in the day and hour of Jupiter, when these planets are in good aspects to one another and are domiciled in a fire sign. He also tells us that the moon must be increasing and the engraving needs to be done in the hour of Mercury. However, my own consideration on this is that, whilst this is a useful approach, it is not the only method of construction which we can consider.

Firstly tin, being of the nature of Jupiter, is an easy metal to work with and being soft will melt on an open flame. The molten metal can be poured out into a mould to make a small round disk. You will need to note that molten metal will be hot so care is needed not to burn yourself or anyone else, so wear goggles and warm the mould so that it is dry before it receives the molten metal. Pure tin ingots can be purchased from eBay and the like. If you do this bear in mind that when metals are molten they are in a sensitive state to the psyche of the operator so one must be in the right frame of mind for the success of the work as they can absorb at this point any negative emotion detrimental to the success of the working.

Also perform this work on a waxing moon, when the Sun and Jupiter behold one another by trine or sextile. Be careful that neither are in a debilitating state. Let the moon also favour the working, by beholding the planets in question, by trine or sextile to one or both of the planets. Trine to both would be preferable as you would have a Grand Trine which is always strong and desirable. If not, let her be moving through one of their houses. The disk can now be engraved with the design. If you are considering drawing the talisman on parchment or paper then you must note to the astrological considerations as you are endeavouring to capture the planetary currents and imprint them on the seal, so your will can make manifest. On the back of the talisman engrave or write the following from Psalm 91:

> *'You will tread on the lion and the adder*
> *The young lion and the serpent you will trample under foot.'*

Having created the talisman, we can empower it accordingly with the use of the following ritual and the names that appear around the seal. These are as follows El, which is at the top of the seal meaning God. Then Elohim meaning God plural. The next name which is half Hebrew letters and English is Elohim Tzabaoth, although the letter T has been dropped meaning God of Hosts. Which is associated with the Kabbalistic sephira Hod. Elion meaning God as does Eserchie. Next name is again half Hebrew and English lettering which says Yod Heh Adonay Adonai meaning Lord and the Yod Heh is probably meant to be YHVH. Lastly Tetragrammaton Saday. Tetragrammaton meaning the four-lettered name i.e. YHVH Saday should I feel be Tzaddai, meaning Holy Lord.

However, whilst Cross-Smith makes the claim that the charm belongs to the Mercurii, its idea can quite clearly be seen in Barratt's work The Magus part II.

Here Barrett says:

> *'If a pentacle were to be made to gain victory, or revenge against one's enemies, as well visible as invisible, the figure must be taken out of the Book of the Maccabees. That is to say, a hand holding a golden sword drawn, about which let there be written the vesicle there contained, to wit.*
>
> *Take the Holy Sword the gift of God wherewith thou shalt slay the adversaries of my people Israel.'*

Barrett also says that the following lines from Psalm 5 can be used instead.

> *'in this is the strength of thy arm.*
> *Before thy face there is death.'*

Curiously, in the work *'Secrets of Solomon: A Witches Handbook from the Venetian Inquisition'* (edited and translated by Joseph H. Peterson), we can see the same idea being presented. It suggests that a seal is created based upon ideas in the Book of Macabees, it also suggests the use of the same wording that the charm contains as given by Cross-Smith. So did the Mercurii take the idea from Barrett? Or did they have the idea from the Venetian material? Or indeed did Barrett have access to the Venetian grimoire? Whatever its origins it is something that is old and has built up its own momentum over time.

Having confected the body of your talisman, create an altar with a white cloth and candles. Let the incense be frankincense. Perform the Q/C as previously.

Invoke God with the following or something of your own creation:

'For I invoke thee O Lord of Creation for thy glory flows out never ending...'

State the intent that the talisman is to protect you from all harm wherever it arises and that all bad vibes, from whom or wherever they are from are returned to the perpetrator thereof.

Sprinkle with holy water saying:

'..Let all malignancy and hindrance be cast forth hence from so only the holy and protective power of God may enter herein.'

Holding the seal in the rising incense say:

'Command O God your strength
Confirm O God what you have wrought in us...
For in a by thy Holy Names
EL: Elohim: Elohim Tzbaoth:
Tzabaoth:

Elion: Eserchie: Adonay:
YHVH: Tetragrammaton Saday:
That thou lettest them be like dust before the wind
and let the angel of the Lord hem them in.
Let their paths become dark and slippery
and may the angel of the Lord pursue them!'

Take the holy oil and mark the talisman with a cross and declare:

'This talisman is dedicated, consecrated and empowered to protect me for all of my days and to return to those who would wish ill unto me that which they would happen unto I.
So Mote It Be!'

Give thanks unto God and to the Holy Names invoked to aid you in this your act of magic. Close with the Q/C.

This simplified rite can of course be made more complex if felt necessary or as one's sense of the arte demands. But whichever way you approach this working when the planets are again in a suitable position repeat the work as this will over time enhance its powers to keep working for you.

One further charm which will be of interest in the following which can be found in Reginald Scott's Elizabethan work 'Discoverie of Witchcraft.'

This talisman has enjoyed a significant popularity at one time as I have found eight surviving copies of it in several Welsh archives… No doubt there are still those which are 'entombed' in various properties in the principality. It has also been used with the Abra Cadabra charm which we explored previously.

PROTECTIVE CHARM FROM THE *DISCOVERIE OF WITCHCRAFT*

The following caption is on the back of the charm:

*'Who so beareth this sign about him,
let him fear no foe, but fear God.'*

This charm also appears in the Book of Oberon, an Elizabethan magical manuscript which has been found in an Oxford archive, indicating that this seal was circulating among the Elizabethan occult world. It is ideal for etching upon a brass disk as the wording can be written on the back and etched, although of course one can create it on paper. I would suggest that you use a full moon for this working…..perhaps a martial or solar hour too as it is a charm created to protect someone or something.

Take the seal and after performing the Q/C and an invocation of God:

'For thee I invoke O Lord of Creation
for thy Glory flows out neverending.'

State the intent of the work which is that the seal will protect the bearer from all fear and harm.

With the following invocation God is invoked to empower the seal:

'Hear me O Lord of Creation Hear me!
For thou how art the maker of all
And to whom all things return
Thee, Thee I invoke.
For thou who art all things and art expressed in all things
Yet naught but silence can express thy nature
Hear Me!
For I invoke thine aid by all that has been,
By all that is and by all that will be.
That this seal is blessed and consecrated by thy Holy Power
and that the bearer hereof will be protected by thy might
from all fear and all harm that may befall them
and that thou wilt bring them safely and securely through
all trials and travails with which they are challenged.
Hear Me O Lord and let my will make manifest accordingly!
So Mote It Be!

Sprinkle with holy water and declare:

'Let all malignancy and hindrance be cast forth hence from
so that only the holy and protecting power of the Most High
may enter herein'

Holding in the rising incense read Psalm 91:

'He who dwells in the shelter of the Most High
Who abides in the shadow of the Almighty,
will say to the Lord… 'My refuge and my fortress
My God in whom I trust.'
For he will deliver you from the snare of the fowler
And the deadly pestilence
He will cover you with his pinions
And under his wings you will find refuge
His faithfulness is a shield and buckler
You will not fear the terror of the night
Nor the arrow that flies by day
Nor the pestilence that stalks in the darkness
Nor the destruction that waste at noonday.
A thousand may fall at your side
Ten thousand at your right hand
But it will not come near you.
You will only look with your eyes
And see the recompense of the wicked.
Because you have made the lord your refuge
The Most High your habitation
No evil shall befall you
No scourge come near your tent.
He will give his angels charge of you
To guard you in all your ways.
On their hands they will bear you up
Lest you dash your foot against a stone.
You will tread on the lion and the adder
The young lion and serpent you will trample under foot.
Because he cleaves to me in love
I will deliver him.
I will protect him because he knows my name.
When he calls to me I will answer him
I will be with him in trouble
I will rescue him and honour him.
With long life I will satisfy him
And show him my salvation.'

Take the talisman and mark a cross on the front of it and as God breathed into Adam's nostrils to bring him to life, so you to will breathe upon the seal declaring:

'Breath of my breath for I give thee life of my life.
For who so beareth this sign about him
Let him fear no foe
But fear God.'

The talisman is now consecrated and empowered. The breathing upon the talisman is something you may do upon all talismanic designs that you may create as part of their consecration.

The following working is from a group of French alchemists, and was given to me with the clear instruction that it is not to be used for the mundane and trivial matters of daily life and should only be used in important matters or emergencies.

Firstly, via meditation and divination, approach the matter in hand to determine how things stand. Then light a candle and burn a little incense, speak the Words of Power in a most solemn manner and trace a cross in the air after each word:

VAHOS + NOSTRO + BAY + GLOY + APON + AGIA +
AGIOS + HISCHRIROS +

(pause for a few seconds)

AGLA + AGLA = AGLA +

AH – GIH – AH : AH – GIH – OS : HIS – KEE – ROS :

Now state in clear terms the situation that you want help to resolve, in the sure and certain knowledge that the names invoked will answer your call.

Now leave the candle to burn out.

QUIS UT DEUS... WHO IS LIKE GOD

Another working for consideration is the following which uses a talisman that invokes the power of St Michael, again a simple but powerful working particularly for healing or protection. It uses a talisman of the archangel and various biblical verses to create St Michael's own psalm. This has ten verses as the archangel is mentioned ten times in the bible, but not in his name as such. The Hebrew name Michael means 'Who is like God.' Not as a question but more of a statement of fact suggesting that the archangel is like God. Sometimes this is also expressed in Latin as 'Quis Ut Deus.'

Therefore, in the hour of the Sun draw the following seal of the archangel Michael in red ink:

Whilst this could be a complex rite let repetition and intent energize this working. Repetition in ritual, as in a novena, will often assist one's magical will to come to fruition. Therefore, let this simple rite be performed for nine days during the solar hour. (But you only have to draw the seal the once not each time you perform the working.)

Rubric:

Create seal in red ink drawn in the solar hour with focus and intent.

Perform K/C.

General invocation of God and statement of intent.

Consecration and dedication of seal.

Invocation of St Michael.

Close and give thanks.

Having created the seal, we face east and perform the K/C and the following invocation of God:

> *For thee I invoke O Lord of Creation*
> *For thy glory flows out never ending*
> *Let this work find favour with thee*
> *And let my will come to pass*
> *[State Intent]*

Sprinkle the seal with holy water saying:

> *Let all malignancy and hinderance be cast forth hencefrom*
> *And let only all good enter herein.*

Hold in the rising incense smoke saying:

> *For in and by the name of the holy and mighty archangel Michael*
> *let my will (state intent) make manifest accordingly…*

Anoint with holy oil saying:

> *'Quis Ut Deus'*

Now and for the next eight days, making a total of nine days, you hold the seal in the rising incense and recite the following Psalm of St Michael. This is composed of various lines from the bible which uses phrases that ask 'Who is like thee?' or implies that there is none who are.

Say after each verse:

> *'By the Archangel Michael'*
> *Who is like to thee O Lord among the Gods?*
> *Who is like thee glorious in holiness…*
> *Fearful in praises, doing wonders!*

By the Archangel Michael.'
(Exodus 15:11)

'O Lord there is none like thee,
neither is there any God besides thee according to all that we have heard
with our ears.
By the Archangel Michael.'
(Chron I. 17:20)

'Lord God of Israel there is no God like thee in the heaven
nor on the earth.
By the Archangel Michael.'
(Chron 2. 6:14)

'All my bones shall say Lord, Who is like thee?
By the Archangel Michael.'
(Ps. 35:10)

'Many, O Lord, my God are thy wonderful works which thou hast done
and thy thoughts which are towards us...
There is none that can be likened to thee.
By the Archangel Michael.'
(Ps. 40:5)

'Thy righteousness also O God is very high, who hast done great things:
O God who is like thee.
By the Archangel Michael.'
(Ps. 71:19)

'Lord who will be likened to thee? Keep not thou silence O God hold not
thy peace and be not still O God.
By the Archangel Michael.'
(Ps. 83:1)

'Among the Gods there is none like thee O Lord
Neither are there any works like thy works.
By the Archangel Michael.'
(Ps. 86:8)

'For who in the heaven can be compared to the Lord?
Who among the sons of the mighty can be likened to the Lord?
By the Archangel Michael.'
(Ps. 89:6)

> *'Lord God of Hosts who is a strong Lord like to thee?*
> *Or thy faithfulness around thee?*
> *By the Archangel Michael.'*
> (Ps. 89:8)

Repeat the intent of the working and then give thanks to the archangel for their help. Finally recite the following to close the working:

> *'Non nobis Domini non nobis Sed nomini tuo da honorum*
> *Propter benignitatem tuam Propter fide tuam.'*
>
> *(Not unto us O Lord Not unto us*
> *But to you be the glory for your mercy and faith.)*
>
> K/C

Place the seal somewhere safe where it can perform its task unhindered…

CHAPTER FIVE
Of the Lords Who Wander

The 'Lords Who Wander', the seven planets that travel through the night sky, are distant specks of light, but mighty Gods, whose power makes manifest at various levels of our lives, regardless of whether we acknowledge them or not.

It is by the use of traditional signs and symbols that we can access their holy and magical powers.

Writing in her work, *Applied Magic & Aspects of Occultism*, Dion Fortune tells us that:

> *'when our emotion goes out strongly towards an object, we are pouring out a subtle but nevertheless potent form of force. The out pouring force is formulated into a thought form…the mental picture is ensouled by the out poured force and becomes an actuality upon the astral.'*

It is quite clear that an emotional rapport with the work must be developed and expressed as this becomes a driving force which will aid in bringing our will into manifestation. Therefore, one cannot simply perform this work with a detached approach; you must be utterly involved with it at all levels. For it will demand your complete intent and nothing less for success to manifest.

We must appreciate that these ancient symbols will represent a cosmic force and when our minds concentrate upon them it will come into contact with that force. By doing so a channel is created between the individual and the energies which the symbol represents in the world soul. This can result in the individual gaining access to the energy and the force which it expresses. Thus, its powers can be brought to bear upon the varied and various situations and challenges of life. As the book of Genesis makes it quite clear, we are created in the likeness of God therefore those powers which make up God are expressed within ourselves, even if they lie dormant or are not that apparent. It is this which allows us to approach the realms of the Gods, and like Prometheus 'steal their Fire' as we challenge our fate with the very powers of the Gods themselves. No other beings in creation can do this…for it is the fate of man to challenge the Gods, indeed even with their own power. For mankind is not a snivelling wretch, burdened with sin and Christian guilt, but a glorious being made in the image of God and bearing his powers too. Therefore let us not forget how the *Corpus Hermeticum* tells us that:

> *'the human is a godlike living thing,*
> *not comparable to other living things of the earth*
> *but to those in heaven above, who are called Gods.'*

The text goes on to make it quite clear that humans can become equal to the Gods. Indeed, it can be seen that mankind has a special place in creation as the Hermetic concept of God deems that God is creation and is expressed by the created, thus everything is alive and conscious at its own level. For the Hermetic concept sees humans as beings who enjoy a special place in creation.

Which is, that they are divine beings who, whilst inhabiting animal bodies, not only possess the divine spark which is in everything, but also share in God's mind. Therefore, salvation in the form of gnosis can only come from mankind developing its relationship with the divine and expressing their mystical nature via the powers thereof. For by doing so, mankind can know God and that man's knowledge of God is necessary for God's own completion.

Subsequently, the relationship between the Creator and the Created becomes an endless cycle of an intimate expression. It is this destiny which grants mankind their 'right' as it were to wield magical power and to be a player in the Great Game of Life.

For behold the seals, symbols and rituals of the Lords Who Wander…

Shabatti

God Name:	YHVH ELOHIM
Archangel:	Tzaphkiel
Angel:	Cassiel
Planet:	Saturn
Colour:	Black
Incense:	Myrrh, civet. Either or both may be blended and digested in olive oil created in the hour of Saturn.
Office:	Has the power to bind or to banish, and the power over older people. Debt and repayment, agriculture, old houses and property.
	Real estate, death and wills. Promotes stability and concentration.

Planetary seal of Saturn:

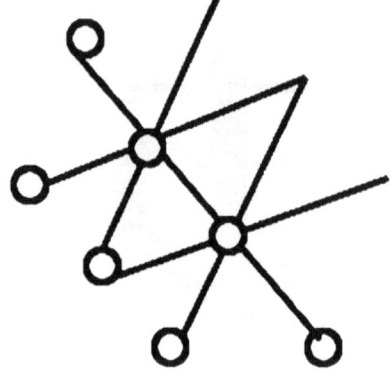

Seal of Binding:

Seal of Banishment:

To bind or to banish someone or a situation is not something to be done on a whim and you will want to give some thought to the situation. However, once your mind is made up there can be no going back.... So be certain.

On a waning moon, and better when Luna is in opposition to Saturn, although a square aspect will suffice and if this is also not possible the working may be done when Luna is domiciled in Capricorn or Aquarius, you must create your seal during the hour of Saturn. By tracing the individual's name over the planetary square of Saturn as has been shown previously, you draw the sigil of their name on the back of the binding or banishing seal as given here, as this will help to strengthen the link with the working and the individual who is being bound or banished.

Ritual Rubric:

A: Determine the astrology of the ritual working

B: Create talisman

C: Create clean workspace with black altar cloth, candles, saturnine incense

D: LBRP (Lesser Banishing Ritual of the Pentagram) or similar if relevant

E: Consecration of candles, fire, incense, water

F: Creation of magical circle

G: Declare the nature of the working

H: Invocation of God for success of the work

I: Exorcise the talisman with fire and water

J: Invocation of planetary energies

K: Blessing and consecration of talisman

L: Empowering the talisman

M: Display the talisman to the compass points declaring its empowerment

N: Give thanks to the Holy Names of God

O: Close the ritual

This is the formula for the following talismans and by simply changing names, colours and invocations it can be seen how simple it is to create the necessary planetary rituals for each of the seals given. Note this rite is for Saturn.

Let the working top be covered in a black cloth and in the middle place the seal of Saturn. Stand a black candle on the seal.

Having performed the LBRP consecrate the salt and water as follows

Trace a cross over the salt saying:

'May wisdom abide in this salt and may it preserve
my mind and body from all corruption.
May all phantoms depart from it
so that it may become a heavenly salt,
salt of earth and earth of salt.
May it feed the threshing ox and strengthen
my hope with the horns of the Winged Bull.
So Mote It Be!'

As you say this hold the palm of your hand over the salt and visualise light pouring from it into the salt and quickening it.

With a little ash from incense in a separate dish, repeat the gestures with your hand and say:

'May this ash return unto the fount of Living Water
may it become a fertile earth and may it bring forth the Tree of Life.'

Add the salt to the ash.

Both the ash and salt are now added to the water saying as you do so:

'In the salt of eternal wisdom in the water of preparation
in the ash whence the new earth springeth be all things accomplished
unto the Ages of Ages.
So Mote It Be!'

Consecration of the Fire

Having lit the charcoal pronounce the following over the glowing embers:

'For I exorcise thee O Creature of Fire by him through whom
all things have been made so that every kind of phantom

*may retire from thee and be unable to harm or deceive in any way,
through the invocation of the Most High Creator of All.*

*Bless O Lord All Powerful and All Merciful, this creature of fire
so that being blessed by Thee, it may for the honour and glory
of thy most Holy Name, so that it may work no hindrance or evil
unto those who use it.
Through thy most Holy Name.
Amen.'*

Over the incense pronounce the following:

*'Hear me O Almighty God…deign to bless these odoriferous spices
so that they may receive strength, virtue and power
to attract the good spirits and to banish and to cause to retire
all hostile phantoms. Through thee O Most Holy Adonai
Who livest and reignest unto the Ages of Ages.
Amen.'*

However if using an incense for a negative working use the following wording instead of the above:

'ADONAI – LAZAI – DALMAI – AIMA – ELOHI

*O Holy Father grant unto us succour, favour and grace
by the Invocation of thy Holy Name so that these things may serve us for aid
in all that we wish to perform therewith that all deceit may quit them and
that they may be blessed and sanctified through thy name.
Amen.'*

Any candles that used in the working will need to be sprinkled with the holy water and held in the rising incense whilst you say:

*'I exorcise thee O creature of wax by him who hath alone
created all things by his word and by the virtue of him
who art pure truth that thou cast out from thee
every phantasm, perversion and deceit of the enemy
and may the virtue and the power of God enter herein
so that thou mayest give us light and chase far from us
all fear and terror.
Amen.'*

Take the holy water and sprinkle around the edge of your circle space, deosil, saying as you do:

'By the power of these holy waters

I bind this circle space from all hindrance and malignancy to this work.'

Cense the circle by taking the censer around the boundary deosil saying:

*'I purify this sacred space with the holy perfumes of the arte
Let it be blessed, dedicated and consecrated unto the success of this mine act of magic.'*

Facing east, perform Q/C and go to the eastern boundary of your circle, pointing your wand or the first two fingers of your right hand at the circumference and tracing a brilliant white light around the circle saying:

*'Nam et prophetas instantissime te O circulo est potentia
ex sanctorum nominibus YHVH ELOHIM
et per vim sancti archangel TZAPHKIEL
et per ARALIM et potestatum SHABBATI
ut quae potestate et suscitabo est apud te est
Victoria hoc operandi de artis.'*

This is an English equivalent which can be used instead:

*'I conjure thee O circle of power by the holy names YHVH ELOHIM
And by the might of the holy archangel TZAPHKIEL
That the mighty ARALIM and the power of SHABBATI
shalt contain the power that I shall raise within thee
for the success of this operation of the arte.'
'Ego me circumcingo virtute horum nominum quibus
hic Circulus est consignatus.'*

The Latin words meaning, 'For I surround myself with the virtue of these names with which this circle is sealed.'

Invoke God for aid in the working:

*'For I invoke thee O Lord of Creation
For thy glory flows out never ending
Be with me now as I perform this work
Which I dedicate wholly unto thee.'*

Trace the Saturnine hexagram in the air over the seal and state the intent of the working.

Then invoke Saturn with the following invocation, letting your gaze be upon the seal of Saturn before you:

'For thee I invoke O Shabbati by the might of the Holy Names
YHVH ELOHIM…… Lord God
Thou who art silence….
For in the darkness I call thee!
As I invoke thee by thy sacred emblems….
By the power of the yoni, The Ark and the Dark Stormy Sea.
I invoke Thee by thy Black Robe of Concealment,
And the Power of Silence and of the Night
that thou (state intent) according to my holy will.'

Gazing into the flame of the black candle before you, see the spirits of Saturn arise via their traditional imagery of The Dark Mother, an old woman upon a crutch, an owl, a black garment hanging in the air and a bearded man.

When they are present take up the talisman and sprinkle with consecrated water and say:

'Let all malignancy and hindrance be cast forth
So that only the holy powers of Shabbati may enter herein.'

Hold the seal in the rising incense saying:

'Hear me O XYZ….
Be thou banished/bound (and see this) in every way
Hear my words I address to thee
For this my will So Mote It Be!

Visualise the form of Saturn as a dark figure, black robed and silent forming around you as you endeavour to identify with this God energy.

Now declare:

> *'I am he Lord of Time*
> *I am He the Silence*
> *I am he the dark dread of night*
> *I am he the Lord of Confinement*
> *I am he who banisheth and doth bind*
> *I am he restricts and who giveth form*
> *For the Lord of Time is my Name.'*

The seal is anointed with consecrated Saturn oil and as you do so declare, if it is a working of binding and confinement the following:

> *'For by the names Schemes Amathai*
> *which Joshua called upon*
> *and the Sun stood still….. I bind thee O XYZ!*

If however you are working a banishment spell then use the following invocation:

> *'Et Minavit eos sicut stipulam ante faciem venti.'*

Meaning, 'For he drove them as chaff before the wind.'

Pour the Saturnine energies into the seal and see your will coming to pass, knowing that it is now fixed. Display the seal at each of the compass points declaring your will, starting in the east and going widdershins (that is against the sun) if binding or banishing.

> *'Take note O ye powers of the East that this seal*
> *is duly consecrated according to my Holy Will*
> *that (state intent) may come to pass as I do so will.*
> *So Mote It Be'*

Repeat at each of the compass points changing the wording regarding each direction that you are facing.

Give thanks to the powers of Saturn and unto God in your own words or use the following formula:

> *'Unto thee O God creator of all things do I give thanks*
> *for the success of this holy work.'*
> *Furthermore I do give thanks unto the holy name of God*
> **YHVH ELOHIM**
> *And unto the mighty archangel Tzaphkael*
> *And of the angels of Aralim and of Shabbati*

For assisting me with this my holy act of magic.'

The license to depart is given saying:

'I now set free any spirit imprisoned by this ceremony
Go in peace unto thine abodes and habitations
and let the blessing of the God Most High be upon thee and about thee.
Furthermore, let there be peace, grace and harmony between thee and me now
and for always.
So Mote It Be.'

The seal can now be placed somewhere safe to do its work undisturbed. If you intend to place it in a freezer or bury it in the churchyard then this is to be done in the saturnine hour, in the sure and certain knowledge that the fate invoked can have no escape. For other planetary workings, use this formula but change the invocations and colours accordingly. It will be of great assistance if you write the ritual out, particularly as this will help to connect with the working.

Tzedek

God Name:	EL
Archangel:	Tzadkiel
Angel:	Sachiel
Planet:	Jupiter
Colour:	Blue
Incense:	Cedar oil mixed with gum copal, grains of paradise, orris, saffron.
	The oil of Jupiter can be made by infusing these herbs in olive oil for a month.
	Mixed in the hour of Jupiter.
Office:	Has the power over bankers, creditors, money, long journeys, clerics, banks, law and spirituality.

Seal of Jupiter:

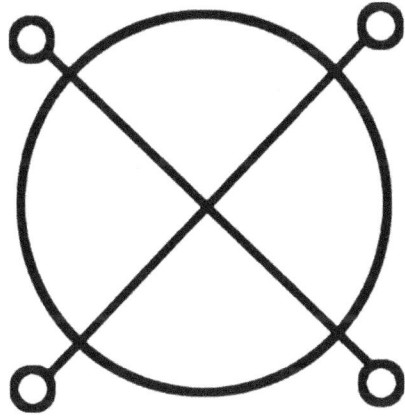

Seal for material wealth and gain:

On the back of this seal you should write the following verse from Psalm. 112:3:

> *'Opes et divitiae in domo eius et Justitia eius manet in aeternum.'*
> *'Wealth and riches are in his house and his righteousness endureth forever.'*

Seal for good luck:

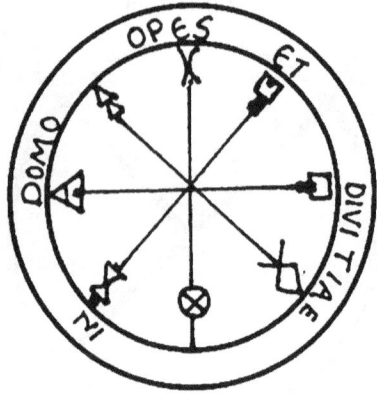

'Dominus meus pastor est et nihil mihi deerit.'
The Lord is my shepherd I shall not want.

Ritual for consecration of the Jupiter seal

Having created the seal for your work and conjured the circle as the arte demands with the formula given (but of course changing the names and colours accordingly, that is by using the God Name EL, Archangel Tzadkiel, Angelic Order Chasmalim, and the name of the planetary energy Tzedek), let the boundary of the circle be stabilised by fire and water as given previously. Jupiter can be invoked with the following invocation and the tracing in the air before you of the Jupiter hexagram:

Thee I invoke O Tzedek by the might of the Holy Name
EL

Thou who art divine and wonderful
For thou who art benevolence and majesty, thee I invoke
and by the might of the Holy Archangel Tzadkiel…
thou who art the Watcher of God
that the Chasmalim, those who art the Bright Shining Ones
make manifest the powers of Tzedek as I do will.'

State the intent of the working.

Consecrate seal with fire and water by sprinkling the seal with water saying:

'Let all malignancy and hindrance be cast out forthwith
So only the holy power Tzedek may enter herein.'

Hold the seal in the rising incense smoke saying:

'Hear me O Tzedek for this charge I lay
Let XYZ happen in every way.
Hear my words that I address to thee
For this my will so mote it be!'

Gaze into the blue candle standing on the seal of Jupiter and see the spirits of Jupiter in the candle flame appear in their traditional forms as a king with a drawn sword riding upon a stag. A man wearing a mitre and a long robe. A young girl with a laurel crown adorned with flowers. A bull, a stag, a peacock. A blue garment, a sword or a box tree.

When you have done this, you must now endeavour to build around you the form of Jupiter, an enthroned king bearing a sceptre and orb in his hands… If this is too much then simply flood your aura with a deep blue colour and imagine this egg-shaped aura of blue around you. As you do so declare the following:

'I am he the majestic one
I am he who didst create the wealth of earth
and the joy in heaven
For mine is the symbol of the equal-armed cross
And the virtue of obedience
For I am king… I am the emperor
The orb of gold and the jewelled sceptre these art mine own.'

Anoint the seal with the oil of Jupiter and recite the lines which go with the seal that you are working with. Then pour the energy into it and see your will coming to pass. Display the seal at the compass points declaring your holy will.

Pass to the east and hold up the seal to the eastern quarter saying:

> *'Behold the seal of Jupiter*
> *Consecrated to my will that XYZ*
> *maketh manifest as I do declare.'*

Repeat at S.W.N., changing the wording accordingly.

Then give thanks unto God and the powers of Jupiter for assisting you in the manifestation of your will in the sure and certain knowledge that, that which you have willed will come into being, for there can be no other outcome:

> *'Therefore, I do give thanks unto Almighty God the maker of all things.*
> *and unto that Mighty Name of God EL….Divine and Wonderful*
> *and of that holy archangel Tzadkiel*
> *and of the Chasmalim and of the holy powers of Tzedek*
> *for assisting me with this my holy act of magic.'*

License to depart:

> *'I now release any spirits that have become imprisoned by the ceremony*
> *Go in peace unto thy abodes and habitations*
> *and let the blessings of the God Most High*
> *be with thee now and for always*
> *SMIB.'*

Madim

God Name:	Elohim Gibor
Archangel:	Kharmael
Angel:	Zamael
Planet:	Mars
Colour:	Red
Incense:	Pepper, Dragon's blood, opopanax: blend in olive oil to create an oil of Mars done during the hour thereof.
Office:	Protect or destroy, banishment and removal, to create hostility and anger, energy, increase life force, vitality and will power.

Seal of Mars:

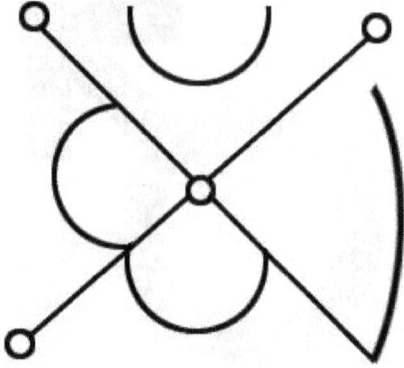

Seal of Chastisement:

The following lines from psalm 105:32:

*'Dedit pluvias eorum grandinem ignem flammanten
in terra eorum et percussit vineas eorum et ficulneas eorum.*

*'He gave them hail for rain and flaming fire in their land
He smote their vines and their fig trees.'*

Seal granting victory in any adversarial situation:

'Dominus a dextris tuis confregit in die irae suae.'
'The Lord at thy right hand shall wound even kings in the day of his wrath.'

Ritual for the consecration of the Mars seal

Having conjured your circle using the following details: God Name Elohim Gibor, Archangel Karmael, Angelic Order Seraphim and the name of Mars Madim, sanctify the boundary with fire and water as given.

Pray to God for success of the working using the wording previously given elsewhere or something of your own devising.

Consecrate seal with fire and water as previously.

Trace the hexagram of Mars over the seal while reciting the following invocation to Mars:

'Thee I invoke O Mars by the Mighty and Powerful name

Elohim Gibor
Thou who art Almighty God!
And by the strength of thy Holy Archangel Kharmael
Who is the Burner of God
That the Seraphim those holy angels of Mars
Wilt make manifest those mighty powers of the Madim
as I do so will.'
(State intent of the working)

Gaze into the flame of the red candle standing upon the planetary seal of Mars and see the shapes of the martial spirits in the flickering light: A mighty king who rides upon a wolf, an armed man, a horse, a red garment. A woman bearing a shield on her arm, a clipping of wool.

When you feel the energies abound let your aura fill with the colour red or better still build the form of a mighty king around yourself.

And declare the following invocation of Mars:

'I am he… The Mighty Warrior
I am he the crimson and the scarlet
and the Great God of War…
I am he who destroys and grants victory
For mine is the scourge and the chain, the sword
and the sharp… sharp point…
For I am courage and I am energy
For I am the power to get things done!

Anoint the seal with the holy oil of Mars and pour the energies aroused into the seal… seeing your will coming to pass.

Say:

'I declare that in and by the Holy Names
ELOHIM GIBOR
And of the mighty archangel Karmael
That the Seraphim those holy angels of Madim
Do cause XYZ in accord with my holy will.
For hear my words that I address to thee
This my will.
So Mote It Be!'

Now display the charged and consecrated seal at the four quarters declaring your will. Give thanks to God and the energies of Mars, licensing them to depart causing no harm nor fear to you and yours, using the following or wording of your own choosing.

Display the seal to the east and declare:

'O Ye powers of the east behold the symbol of my holy will
That makes manifest according to mine intent.'

Repeat at S.W.N. changing directions accordingly.

Close ritual with the following or something of your own devising:

'I give thanks unto God for the success of this work
may the glory be thine for always.
Unto those mighty names of God Elohim Gibor
And the holy archangel Karmael
And the Seraphim, those mighty angels of the Madim
Unto thee do I give thanks.
Therefore, let there be peace grace and harmony between us now and for
always as thou departest unto thy realms and habitations.
SMIB.'

Keep the seal safe and out of sight.

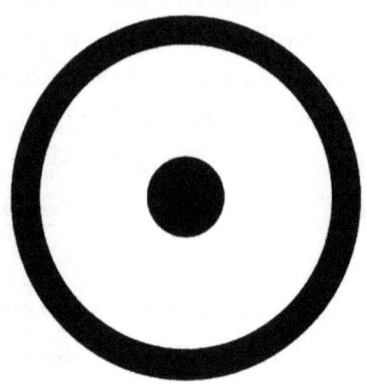

Shemesh

God Name:	YHVH Aloah-Va-Daath
Archangel:	Mikael
Angel:	Nakhiel
Planet:	Sun
Incense:	Frankincense, cinnamon can be blended in olive oil to create an oil thereof done in the solar hour.
Colour:	Gold
Office:	Healing, gaining of money or favours from those in authority, protection, enlightenment, promotion of peace and harmony.

Seal of the Sun:

Seal of good fortune and success:

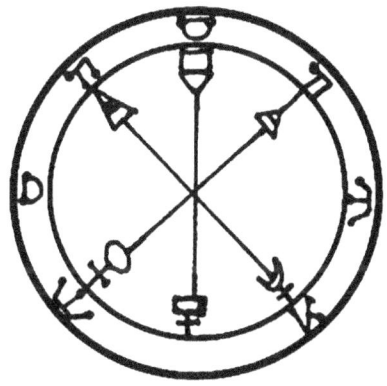

*'Regnum omnium saeculorum
et domination ab aetate ad aetatem'*

*('My kingdom is an everlasting kingdom
and my dominium endureth from age unto age')*

For healing and the promotion of wellbeing:

Invocation to be recited during the consecration of the seal:

*'Custodi animam meam quoniam
sanctus sum salvum fac servum tuum qui sperat in te.'*

'Preserve my life for I am godly save thy servant who trusts in thee.'

As previously, write these words upon the reverse of the seal as their recitation is part of the consecration and the empowering of the talisman. Follow the formula given and change the names and colours accordingly.

Ritual for consecration

Construction of circle using God Name YHVH ALOAH VE-DAATH, Archangel Mikael, Angelic Order Malakim, and Shemesh the Sun.

Again, define the boundary with fire and water.

Pray to God for the success of the working:

*'Holy art thou Lord of Creation for thy power flows out
Unto the end of creation rejoicing...'*

Trace solar hexagram and intone the following invocation of the solar energies:

*'Hear me O Sol, for Thee I invoke
Thou who art the giver of all life and the sustainer thereof
Hear Me!
For I invoke thy mighty powers by the Holy Names
YHVH ALOAH VA DAATH
God who art manifest in the sphere of the mind
For invoke the lifegiving powers of the Sun by the name of the mighty*

> *Archangel Mikael!*
> *That by the powers of the Malakim*
> *The power of Shemesh the Sun maketh manifest as I do will!'*

Watch the flame of the candle which you have placed upon the planetary seal upon the altar and see the spirits of the Sun congregate therein… taking the form of a crowned king, a lion, a queen with a sceptre, a cock bird, or golden garment.

Consecrate the seal as previously performed with fire and water.

Visualise around yourself the form of an enthroned and crowned king or a brilliant golden colour.

Recite the following invocation as the imagery takes over:

> *'I am he, the great giver of life*
> *I am he who sustaineth all things*
> *For I am he, the rose cross, the cube and the lamen*
> *For I am he, the beauty and the harmony*
> *I am he, the harmony of creation…*
> *Therefore, by these names let the powers of Shemesh*
> *make manifest according to my holy will.'*

Anoint the seal with the oil of the Sun and see your will coming to pass as you pour the powers invoked into the seal in the sure and certain knowledge that your will…. will come to pass.

Close the working by displaying the seal at the compass points starting in the east and then S.W.N. whilst declaring your intent. Give thanks to God and the powers of the Sun invoked and close the ritual, giving license to depart for any spirits that may have become trapped by this ceremony.

> *'Therefore, I give thanks unto thee O God for the success*
> *of this my holy act of magic.*
> *And unto those holy names YHVH ALOAH VA-DAATH*
> *And of the archangel Mikael*
> *And of the Malakim that the powers of Shemesh*
> *make manifest as I do will.*
>
> *SMIB*

Nogah

God Name:	YHVH Tzabaoth
Archangel:	Haniel
Angel:	Anael
Planet:	Venus
Colour:	Green
Incense:	Rose, benzoin, red sandal, and musk can be blended as an oil for the work.
Office:	All acts of pleasure, love and friendship, good luck and creativity.

Seal of Venus:

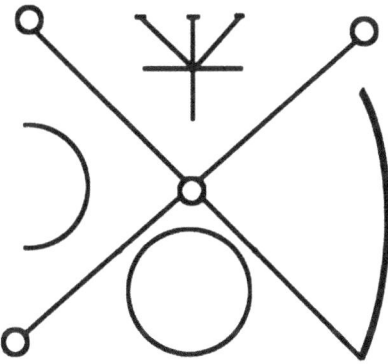

Seal for Love:

'Et duo in carne una.'
'and they were one flesh.'

Seal for Good Luck:

'*Stercore erigens pauperem de stercore
erigens pauperum ut collocet eum cum principibus
cum principibus populi sui.*'

'*Lifting up the poor out of the mire and raising the needy from the dunghill
that he may set him with princes even with the princes of his people.*'

Consecration of Venus seal

Trace hexagram:

Invocation of Venus

*Hear Me, O Lady of Mystery and Delight
For Thee I invoke. Thou vision of Beauty Triumphant
For Thee I invoke by the mighty name of God
YHVH TZABAOTH
Leader of Armies is thy name.*

> *For I invoke thee, the power of Love and Delight*
> *By the name of the Holy Archangel Haniel*
> *Thou who art the Grace of God*
> *That the holy Elohim may make forth the manifestation*
> *of the powers of Nogah as I do will...'*

Watch the flame of the green candle and let the imagery of Venus build up. See the traditional imagery of Venus - the rose, a king with a sceptre upon a camel, a naked girl, a female goat, a camel, a dove or a green garment.

Again, consecrate the seal as previously changing names and colours appropriately.

Let the imagery of Venus build around you as the naked woman... Or flood your aura with the colour green and recite the following invocation:

> *'For I am She... Beauty Triumphant*
> *I am She... the Green of Nature*
> *I am She... who art the power of thy Loins,*
> *thy Hips and thy Legs*
> *I am She... who art sensuosity*
> *For, The Lamp, The Girdle and The Rose for these art mine*
> *For it is I... who art the power of thy sexuality.'*

Anoint the seal with the oil of Venus and pour the power into the seal as you see your will coming to pass. Close the working by displaying the seal at the compass point starting in the east:

> *'Hear me, O ye mighty powers of the east*
> *For this seal is duly consecrated unto my holy will that*
> *XYZ may make manifest as I do will.'*

Repeat at the S.W.N.

Having declared the seal is charged according to your will, give thanks to the Holy Names of Venus and unto God declare any spirits trapped by the ceremony are free to leave in peace and harmony.

> *'Therefore, I give thanks unto God*
> *for the success of this Holy Act of Magic*
> *and unto the Mighty Names YHVH TZABAOTH*
> *and the Archangel Haniel and that holy order of angels*
> *the Elohim that the powers of Nogah hath aided me as I do will.*
> *Therefore, depart Ye in peace unto thy abodes and realms*
> *and let the blessings of God the Most High*
> *be with us now and for always.*
>
> SMIB.'

Kokab

God Name:	ELOHIM TZABAOTH
Archangel:	Raphael
Angel:	Mikael
Planet:	Mercury
Colour:	Orange
Incense:	Storax, lavender, fennel, mastic
Office:	Business matters, writing, contracts, communication, buying, selling, travel, information and retrieving stolen goods.

Seal of Mercury:

Seal for the return of stolen goods:

'Ecce turbatio in matutino et non subsistet vespere
Pars eorum qui vastaverunt nos
Et est pars eorum qui vastaverunt nos et sors.'
'At evening time behold terror!
Before morning they are no more!
This is the portion of those who despoil us
and the lot of those who plunder us.'
(Isaiah 17:14)

Hold the seal in the rising incense smoke as you recite the invocation, naming the perpetrator if you know them, otherwise refer to 'Those who have stolen from us.' Or some such wording. Do this in the hour of Mercury, however if you calculate when the moon is in the second house which deals with your moveable goods and money, this would also be useful, although it may not coincide with the Mercury hour. Remember at some point every day the moon will be domiciled in the second house. Repeat this working for three days and if the goods have not been returned by then burn the seal when the moon is making an adverse aspect to Saturn and scatter the ashes outside your front door reading the following invocation:

*'By the Great and Almighty Power of Alpha and Omega,
YHVH and Emanuel, and by him that divided the red sea
and by that great Power that turned all the waters and rivers in Egypt
into blood and turned all the dust into lice and blains
and by the power that brought forth frogs all over the land
of Egypt and entered into all the king's palaces and chambers
and by that Great Power that terrible thunder and lightning
and hailstones mixed with fire and sent locust which did
destroy all green things in the whole land of Egypt
both of man and beast and by that Great Power that divided
the hard rocks and the rivers of water issued out of the same
in the wilderness and by that Great Power
that led the children of Israel out of Egypt into the land of Canaan
and by that Great Power that destroyed Sennacherib's great host
and by the Great and Almighty Power of Him who walketh on the sea
as on the dry land and by that Great and Almighty Power
that raised dead Lazarus out of his grave and by the Almighty Power
of the holy blessed and glorious Trinity that did cast the
devil and all disobedient spirits out of heaven into hell
that thou thief return immediately and restore the goods again
that thou hast stolen away. Therefore, in and by the names
of the Almighty God before rehearsed I charge thou, O thief,
to restore the goods again immediately or else the wrath of God
may fall upon thee
and cause thee to be consumed.
Amen.'*

Seal to promote wisdom and knowledge:

*'Sapientia et virtus in domo sua
et in omni Scientia quae solum
secum auferret usque in sempiternum.'*

*'Wisdom and virtue are in his house and the knowledge
of all things remaineth with him'.*

Consecration of the Mercury talisman

Having created our seal and the circle has been conjured by using the God name Elohim Tzabaoth, Archangel Raphael, Order of Angels Beni Elohim that by the power of Kokab the energies arouse within the circle manifest as we do will.

Sanctify with fire and water and pray to God for the success of the working for without whose help nothing is possible:

*'Blessed art thou Lord of Creation whose glory flows out neverending
Be with me now as I perform this my holy work.'*

Let the seal be consecrated with fire and water as previously and trace the hexagram of Mercury over the seal and declare:

Invocation of Mercury

'For Thee I invoke O Mercurius
By the Glory and the Splendour
By the might of the Holy Name
ELOHIM TZABAOTH Gods of Hosts.
And in the mighty name of thine archangel Raphael
Healer of God
That the holy Beni Elohim…The Sons of God
Do cause the powers of Kokab to manifest as I do will.'

Watch the flame of the Orange candle and let the images of Mercury build around the flame. See the spirits manifest as King riding upon a bear, A young boy, a woman holding a distaff, a dog, a she-bear and a magpie. Or a garment that changes colour. When the energies have been aroused, visualise around yourself the form of the hermaphrodite building up or simply flood your auric field with the colour orange.

Say:

'For mine is the Glory and the Splendour
And the vision thereof
For I am he the hermaphrodite
Who distinguishes between falsehood and truthfulness
For I am reason, I am number, the written word is mine
As is the means thereof….
For mine art the Holy Names, the apron and the cubic stone
For the messenger of the Gods am I.'

Anoint the seal with the oil of Mercury and pour the energy into the seal and see you will it coming to pass. The display as you previously did the seal at the four compass points declaring your intent. Close with thanks unto God and those energies of Mercury and the license to depart.

I give thanks unto God the Most High
for aiding me with this mine act of magic.
Furthermore, I give thanks unto the holy names ELOHIM TZABAOTH
and unto the mighty archangel Raphael and the holy Beni Elohim
And the powers of KOKAB for aiding me thus.
Therefore depart Ye in peace unto thy proper realms and habitations and let the blessings of the God Most High be with thee now and for always.

SMIB.

Levanah

God Name:	Shaddai El Chai
Archangel:	Gabriel
Angel:	Gabriel
Planet:	Moon
Colour:	White, Silver or Purple
Incense:	Jasmine, White Sandalwood, Camphor, Lotus, Lignum aloes
Office:	All things relating to women, scrying, psychic matters, domesticity, children, growth, journeys by water, the sea, pregnancy, and clairvoyance.

Seal of the Moon:

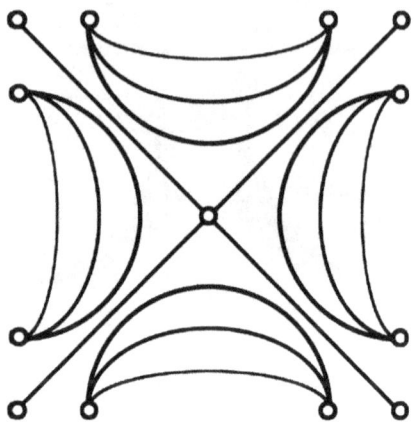

Seal for clairvoyance and psychism:

*'Angelus qui loquebatur in me et dixit ad me leva
oculos tuos et vide quid est hoc quod egreditur.'*

*'Then the angel who talked with me came forward and said unto me
Lift your eyes and see what this is that goes forth.'*
Zechariah 5:1

Seal for the promotion of domestic stability:

'Et misericordia tua subsequetur me
Omnibus diebus vitae meae
Et ut inhabitem in domo Domini
In longitudinem dierum.'

'But thy loving kindness and mercy
shall follow me all the days of my life.
And I will dwell in the house of the Lord forever.'
Psalm 23:6

Consecration of the Luna seals

Having created our seal as the arte demands let us create our circle and use the names of Luna to ward it. Let the circle be conjured by the God Name Shaddai El Chai, the Archangel Gabriel and the Order of Angels Ishim and by the power of Levanah the moon. Take fire and water as before around the circle's boundary marking the space. Invoke God to aid you in your undertaking:

'Blessed art thou Lord of Creation whose glory flows out never-ending.'

Trace the Luna hexagram over the seal and invoke the Luna energies with this invocation or one of your own devising:

Invocation of Luna

'Thee I invoke O Luna by the Mighty Name SHADDAI EL CHAI
Thou who art the Queen of the Night
For Thee I invoke by the holy archangel Gabriel
and by the power of the Ishim
That the might of Levanah aideth me with this my act of magic.
For thee I invoke O Luna thou who art the Queen of the Night
Thou who art foundation and the great rhythm of life
For thine is the ebb and the flow, the subtle tides of creation.'

Watch the flame of the candle that stands upon the planetary seal and see the imagery of the lunar spirits build around the candle flame. These can manifest as huntress with a bow, a deer, a small child, a goose, a cow or a silver garment.

Build around yourself with your imagination the tall woman robed in white with the lunar crescent on her brow. Let the night sky be behind her, alternatively simply imagine that your aura is flooded with a dark purple colour.

Invoke the lunar energies as such:

'I am she who art the Queen of the Night
I am she who art the ebb and flow of the tides of life
I am she who art the foundation of the world
For mine is the mirror and the womb
the perfumes of arte and the sandals thereof
For I grant the Vision of the Machinery of the Universe
and unto thee I give independence too.'

Anoint the seal with the holy oil of Luna created as done with the other planetary oils. Pour the Luna energy into the seal before you and again as with the other seals display at the four compass points starting in the east and travelling S.W.N. Declare that it is charged as your will demands.

Return to the centre of your circle and give thanks and the license to depart:

'For I do give thanks unto thee O God
for thine aid in this my holy magic.
Furthermore I give thanks unto the Mighty Name of God
SHADDAI EL CHAI… the Almighty Living God
And unto the holy archangel Gabriel and the Ishim
For the magical aid of Levanah.
Therefore, depart in peace unto thy proper abodes and habitation
And go with the blessings of the God Most High.'

CHAPTER SIX
Of the Mansions of the Moon

Unless you have studied the *Picatrix* or Agrippa's *Three Books of Occult Philosophy*, you are unlikely to be familiar with the spirits that belong to the Mansions of the Moon. These are a group of 28 lunar spirits with their own office which can help or hinder a wide range of human activity and are indeed relatively easy to work with. However, the means to do so successfully has not been as widely disseminated as it could have been, something which I hope this chapter goes some way to assimilate.

The mansions of the moon are created by starting at 0° Aries and adding on 12°51′ which gives us the first mansion of the moon. If we add on another 12°51′ this will bring us to 25°42′ Aries, creating the second mansion of the moon. This figure is the distance which the moon will travel in a twenty-four hour period. By repeating this around the zodiac we will have the 28 mansions of the moon. Each mansion has an angel with whom we can work with; traditionally it has always had an image which you would have been expected to draw and work with. However I wish to take a different approach with this work and as each mansion of the moon has a name, we can, via the Lunar kamea, create the sigil of each of the Luna mansions.

As far as I am aware this has not been done before and is certainly not in the public domain. Agrippa has given us the names of the angels of each mansion, we know too that by its very name this is Luna magic. Therefore, by the use of the God name and the archangel of the moon we can work with these angels and their potencies. Although the Picatrix does suggest that these mansions are ideally worked with when a series of astrological timings are judicious, this is not always practical and I would suggest that we concentrate on the state of the moon, as this is Luna magic.

Therefore, we will need to work when the moon is domiciled in the mansion we want to work with. However, if it is a benign working, let the moon be free from the affliction of Mars or Saturn, and also let the moon be waxing. Of course, if the working is for an adverse purpose then the reverse will need to apply. Also, the working will need to be performed during the Lunar hour, better still if the mansion of the moon is either in the 1st or 10th house of a chart as it will be strengthened by this position. Having limited the conditions for a successful outcome to what I feel are the basics, the Picatrix does tell us that if we are unable to meet these circumstances and the working is urgent, then let either Jupiter or Venus be either on the ascendant or the mid heaven of the chart for the working, as this will go some way to mitigate the adverse astral conditions which will otherwise hinder the successful outcome of your work.

To quote briefly from Book 5 of the Picatrix chapter 3:

> *'If there should be some very necessary working that cannot possibly wait until the moon is free from all of the aforesaid debilities, place Jupiter and Venus on the ascendant or midheaven because they will rectify an unfortunate moon.'*

The method of working with these seals can be done as follows: we can create scenes from the imagery which has traditionally been associated with each of the mansions and then imagine walking into that scene. That is after performing an invocation of the mansion, something we will consider in the next section, as we can then experience the mansion on its own terms, with something of its mystery perhaps being imparted to you.

Evocation of the angel of each mansion, whilst a more demanding approach, would be highly effective. Regarding the material for such an approach I have written about this praxis extensively elsewhere and the reader can consult with these past works if they wish to study the modus operandi of such an approach. Candle magic would be a simple means of granting ingress unto the potency of each of the mansions; or simply creating a talisman of the mansion that you are endeavouring to work with, as this work is primarily concerned with talismans.

The talismanic sigils have been created from the name of each of the mansions of the moon and can be either drawn in purple or silver ink. They can also be etched on to a silver disc. However to do this, which is highly effective, please consult YouTube on etching silver as it is a little more demanding than the basic etching which this work has covered, as ferric chloride will not etch silver and to be successful a different process has to be administered

Therefore, you must pay attention to the position of Luna in all your workings as she is the foremost of all the planets. For she has the most manifest effect on all things, as she receives the impression and influences of all the planets and the fixed stars. Therefore, she is the mediatrix of all their effects upon earth, thus her strength will accord with the nature of the planetary aspects with which she is conjoined.

I have used the mansion names that are given in the Picatrix, although there are other authorities who will use the Arabic names, and I have also used the Picatrix names for the sigils of each mansion. While each mansion has various powers, their attributes perhaps say something regarding the medieval mindset and some of their properties may not be relevant for today. However, it is quite clear that many of these mansions have a dual personality and indeed some can cause harm as well as aiding the individual in their endeavours.

First Mansion: Alnath

Position:	0°-12°51 Aries
Angel:	Geniel
Incense:	Storax
Office:	This mansion is good to make a journey safely and to return in like manner. Traditionally the mansion when if medication was taken when the moon is domiciled or the mansion is ruling the tenth house of medicine then it would be more effective. However, this mansion is to be worked with to sow discord between couples, friends or allies. Or even to disperse servants.
Meditation imagery:	A dark man wearing a garment of hair that is girdled around. He holds a lance in his right hand.

Seal of Alnath:

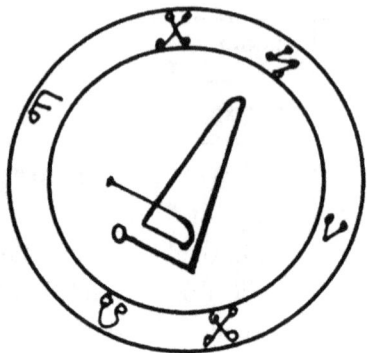

Seal of Geniel:

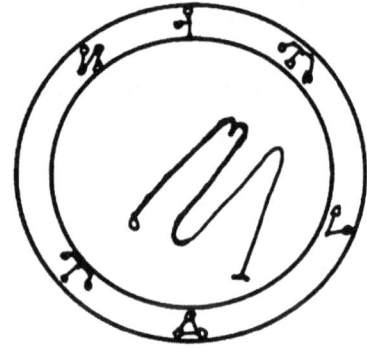

Second Mansion: Albotain

Position:	12°51'- 25°42' Aries
Angel:	Enediel
Incense:	Lignum aloes
Office:	This mansion is good for finding water and for dowsing. It is also good for finding treasure. Wheat or other grain when planted under this mansion will flourish. However, it will also promote discord between people, and the destruction of buildings.
Meditation imagery:	A crowned king seated upon a throne.

Seal of Albotain:

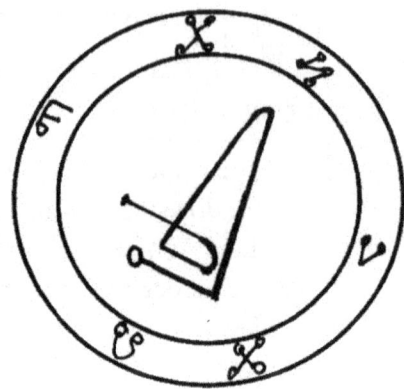

Seal of the angel Enediel:

Third Mansion: Azoraya

Position:	25°42 'Aries - 8°34' Taurus
Angel:	Amixiel
Incense:	Camphor, mastic, musk and aromatic oils
Office:	The third mansion of the moon is good for alchemical works. It is also helpful in promoting a safe sea journey. It is good to cause love between man and woman. It will aid in successful hunting and all works that are done with fire. And it will also keep prisoners incarcerated.
Meditation imagery:	A well-clothed woman sitting in a chair, her right hand held to her head.

Seal of Azoraya:

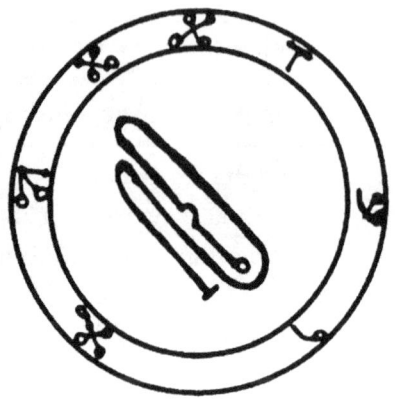

Seal of the angel Amixiel:

Fourth Mansion: Aldebaran

Position: 8°34' - 21°25' Taurus

Angel: Azariel

Incense: Myrrh and storax

Office: This mansion will aid in the destruction of cities and villages, also any other building. It will cause discord between a couple and has been used traditionally to bind venomous beasts. It will hamper those who are seeking treasure.

Meditation imagery: A soldier mounted upon a horse. In his righthand he holds a serpent.

Seal of Aldebaran:

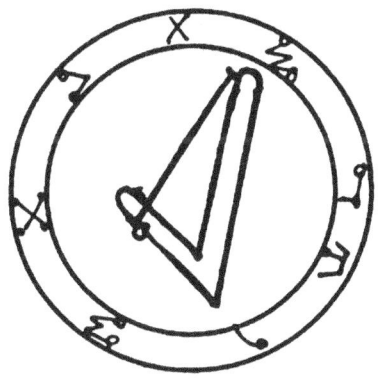

Seal of the angel Azariel:

Fifth Mansion: Almices

Position: 21°25' Taurus - 4°17' Gemini

Angel: Gabiel

Incense: Sandalwood

Office: This mansion is good for the encouragement of learning, particularly among young children. It will also aid sailors and travellers, whilst it can be used to improve buildings and to promote harmony between couples. It can also be used to disrupt the friendship between two people.

Meditation imagery: The head of a man.

Seal of Almices:

Seal of the angel Gabiel:

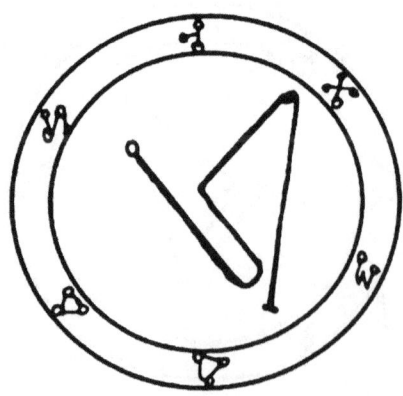

Sixth Mansion: Athaya

Position: 4°17' Gemini - 17°8' Gemini

Angel: Dirachiel

Incense: Lignum aloes and amber

Office: This mansion will work for the destruction of cities and villages, to besiege them with armies and for the enemies of kings to have revenge. Whilst it is not good for medication and will also destroy crops, it is however good for the promotion of friendship between two people.

Meditation imagery: Two people embracing.

Seal of Athaya:

Seal of the angel Dirachiel:

Seventh Mansion: Aldirath

Position: 17°8' Gemini - 0° Cancer

Angel: Scheliel

Incense: Sweet perfumes… vanilla

Office: This mansion of the moon will increase profit from any enterprise and is also good to promote safe travel. It will increase the yield of crops that are grown and it will also promote friendship. Traditionally it has also been used to gain the favour of those who make decisions over you concerning aspects of one's life. However, it has also been used to remove officials and to expel flies.

Meditation imagery: A man richly clothed and holds his hands heavenward as he prays.

Seal of Aldirath:

Seal of the angel Scheliel:

Eighth Mansion: Annathra

Position: 0° - 12°51' Cancer

Angel: Amnediel

Incense: Sulphur

Office: This mansion is good to promote love and friendship, it will also promote the friendship between allies. It will protect those who travel in wagons through the countryside and will also expel bugs and mice. It has the power to destroy and afflict captives should that be deemed necessary.

Meditation imagery: An eagle with the face of a man.

Seal of Annathra:

Seal of the angel Amnediel:

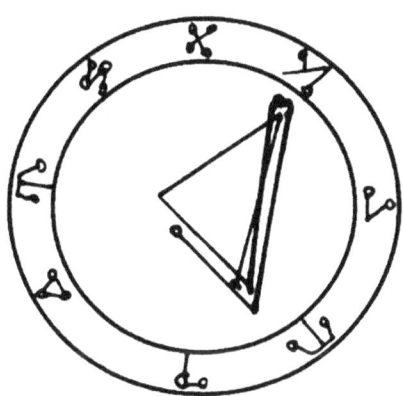

Ninth Mansion: Atarf

Position: 12°51' - 25°42' Cancer

Angel: Barbiel

Incense: Pine resin

Office: This mansion will destroy crops and cause adversity for travellers. It will cause disagreements between allies and friends, but will help you when attacked by another man.

Meditation imagery: A man wanting his privy parts, he has covered his eyes with his hands.

Seal of Atarf:

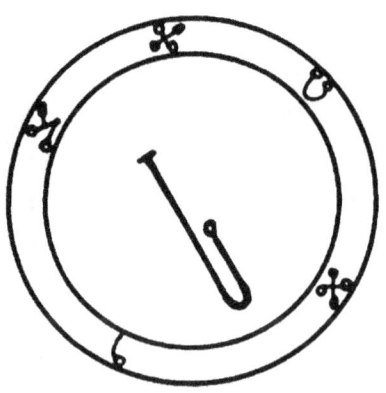

Seal of the angel Barbiel:

Tenth Mansion: Algebha

Position: 25°42' Cancer - 8° 34' Leo

Angel: Ardesiel

Incense: Amber

Office: This mansion is good to promote love between man and woman, but it will also aid you in the destruction of your enemies. It will bring you friendship and aid from allies and friends. It is also good to strengthen buildings.

Meditation imagery: The head of a Lion.

Seal of Algebha:

Seal of the angel Ardesiel:

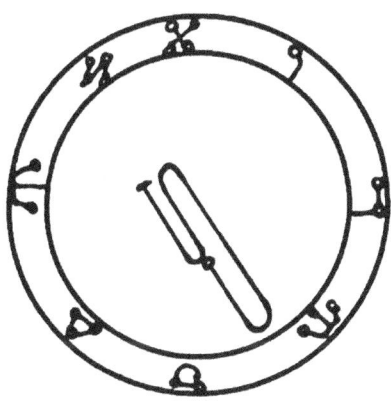

Eleventh Mansion: Azobra

Position: 8° 34' - 21° 25' Leo

Angel: Neciel

Incense: Frankincense

Office: This mansion is traditionally good to rescue people from difficult situations. It is also helpful if laying siege to cities and villages. It promotes trade and profit from any enterprise, and will also aid the traveller in staying safe on their journeys.

Meditation imagery: A man who rides upon a lion, who holds its ear with his right hand.

Seal of Azobra:

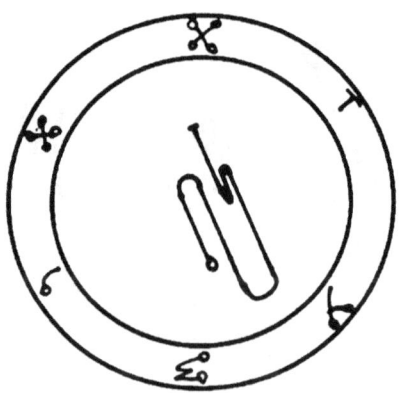

Seal of the angel Neciel:

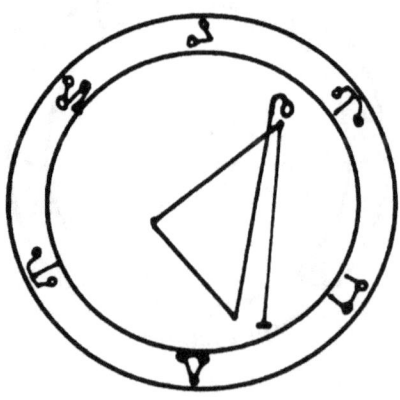

Twelfth Mansion: Acarfa

Position: 21°25' Leo - 4° 17' Virgo

Angel: Abdizuel

Incense: asafoetida

Office: This mansion will increase the yield of crops. Therefore, it would be a good time to plant seed when the moon is domiciled in this mansion. It will also destroy riches and ships, but will however promote steadfastness and reliability in allies, officials and servants.

Meditation imagery: A man fighting a dragon.

Seal of Acarfa:

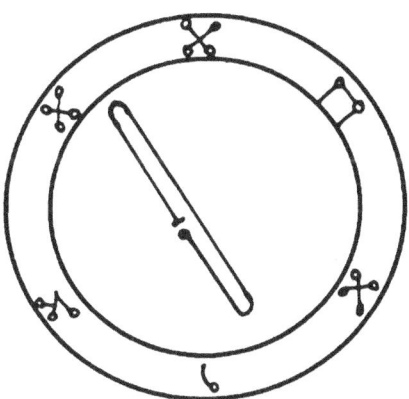

Seal of the angel Abdizuel:

Thirteenth Mansion: Alahue

Position: 4° 17' - 17° 8' Virgo

Angel: Jazeriel

Incense: Amber and Lignum Aloes

Office: Will increase trade and profit. Is also useful to promote good harvests, safe journeys and to gain the good will of those above one in life.

Meditation imagery: An image of a man and a woman embracing.

Seal of Alahue:

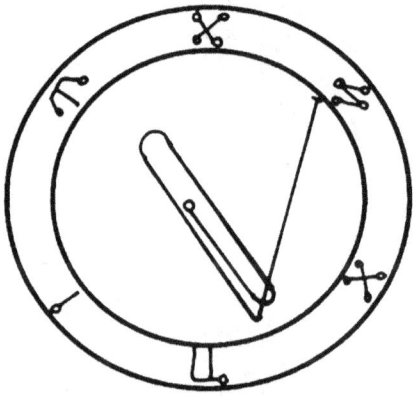

Seal of the angel Jazeriel:

Fourteenth Mansion: Azimech

Position: 17° 8' Virgo 0° Libra

Angel: Ergediel

Incense: Amber and Lignum Aloes

Office: This mansion will promote love and heal the sick, but it will destroy harvests and plants. It will, however, destroy lust and those who travel, but be good for kings and those who sail the seas, and to keep friendships.

Meditation image: A dog who bites its tail.

Seal of Azimech:

Seal of the angel Ergediel:

Fifteenth Mansion Algarfa

Position: 0° - 12° 51' Libra

Angel: Ataliel

Incense: Frankincense and nutmeg

Office: Good for digging wells and seeking treasure that is buried. It will impede travellers and separate couples. It will also cause discord and scatter one's enemies and will destroy their abodes.

Meditation imagery: A man who is sitting and writing a letter.

Seal of Algarfa:

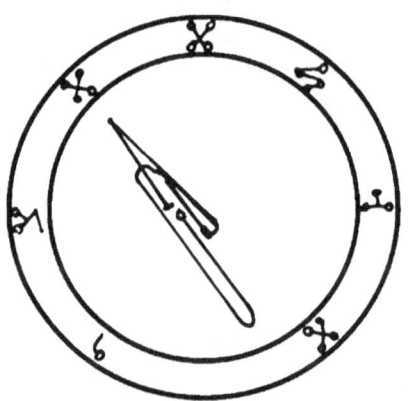

Seal of the angel Ataliel:

Sixteenth Mansion Azubene

Position: 12°51' - 25°42' Libra

Angel: Azaruel

Incense: Sweet spices (suggest cinnamon, nutmeg, cloves)

Office: Has the power to destroy merchandise, harvests and plants. It will create discord between people and between couples. It is good for seduction and will also free captives.

Meditation imagery: A man sitting in a chair who holds a set of scales in his hand.

Seal of Azubene:

Seal of the angel Azaruel:

Seventeenth Mansion: Alichil

Position: 25°42' Libra - 8°36' Scorpio

Angel: Adriel

Incense: Frankincense

Office: This mansion will protect against thieves and robbers.

Meditation imagery: The image of an ape.

Seal of Alichil:

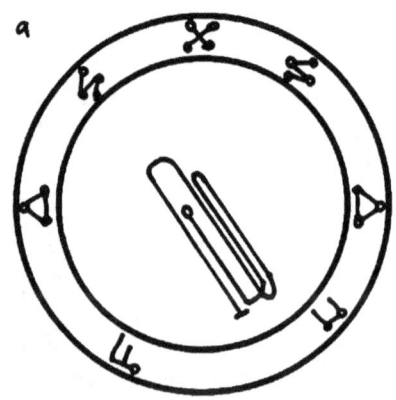

Seal of the angel Adriel:

Eighteenth Mansion: Alcalb

Position: 8°36' - 21°25' Scorpio

Angel: Egibiel

Incense: Antler (I would also suggest something scorpionic such as opponax)

Office: Clears serpents and venomous beasts from an area where it is buried.

Meditation imagery: A snake holding its tail above its head.

Seal of Alcalb:

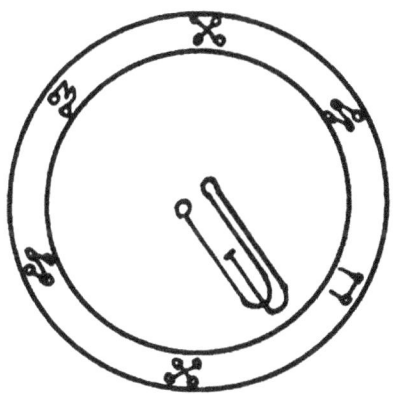

Seal of the angel Egibiel:

Nineteenth Mansion: Exaula

Position: 21°25' Scorpio - 4°17' Sagittarius
Angel: Amutiel
Incense: Storax
Office: For easing childbirth.

Meditation imagery: A woman holding her hands to her face.

Seal of Exaula:

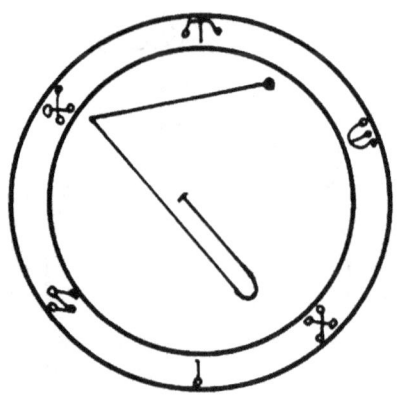

Seal of the angel Amutiel:

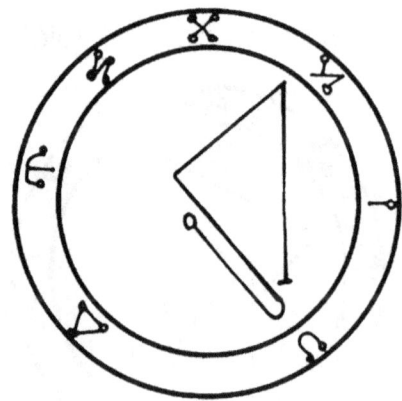

Twentieth Mansion: Nahaym

Position: 4°17' - 17°8' Sagittarius

Angel: Kyriel

Incense: Cedar or violet

Office: Good to promote a successful hunt.

Meditation imagery: A figure which is half-man half-horse.

Seal of Nahaym:

Seal of the angel Kyriel:

Twenty-first Mansion: Elbelda

Position: 17°8' Sagittarius - 0° Capricorn

Angel: Bethnael

Incense: Brimstone

Office: This mansion is worked with to bring ruin and destruction to somebody.

Meditation imagery: A man seated and with two faces looking either-side.

Seal of Elbelda:

Seal of the angel Bethnael:

Twenty-second Mansion: Caadaldeba

Position: 0° - 12°51' Capricorn

Angel: Geliel

Incense: Mastic

Office: Whilst this mansion is good to help cure illness and promote goodwill between allies, it will also help captives to flee, but it can be used to cause discord between two people.

Meditation imagery: A man with winged feet.

Seal of Caadaldeba:

Seal of the angel Geliel:

Twenty-third Mansion: Caaddebolach

Position: 12°51' - 25°42' Capricorn

Angel: Requiel

Incense: Myrrh

Office: Grants healing and will promote peace between two people. However, it can break up relationships if worked with during a waning moon.

Meditation imagery: A cat with the head of a dog.

Seal of Caaddebolach:

Seal of the angel Requiel:

Twenty-fourth Mansion: Caadacohot

Position: 25°42' Capricorn - 8°34' Aquarius

Angel: Abrinael

Incense: Benzoin

Office: Used to increase one's flocks and herds of cattle and other livestock.

Meditation image: A mother feeding her child.

Seal of Caadacohot:

Seal of the angel Abrinael:

Twenty-fifth Mansion: Caaddalhacbia

Position: 8°24' - 21°25' Aquarius

Angel: Aziel

Incense: Cedar

Office: To take enemies captive and to besiege cities and villages. Helps messengers carry information quickly and return. Will also separate couples and destroy harvests. Will bind part of the body so it cannot function and will also strengthen buildings. Agrippa tells us it is useful to preserve trees and harvests if the figure is carved on the wood of a fig tree.

Meditation image: A man planting.

Seal of Caaddalhacbia:

Seal of the angel Aziel:

Twenty-sixth Mansion: Almiquedam

Position: 21°25' Aquarius - 4°17' Pisces

Angel: Tagriel

Incense: Musk, rose

Office: This seal will bind people in love, it will also protect travellers, strengthen buildings and keep prisoners from escaping.

Meditation image: A woman who is washing and combing her hair.

Seal of Almiquedam:

Seal of the angel Tagriel:

Twenty-seventh Mansion: Algarf

Position: 4°17' - 17°8' Pisces
Angel: Alheniel
Incense: Asafoetida and storax
Office: To destroy fountains and baths.

Meditation image: A winged man who holds in his hand a vessel with holes in it.

Seal of Algarf:

Seal of the angel Alheniel:

Twenty-eighth Mansion: Arrexhe

Position: 17°8' Pisces - 0° Aries

Angel: Amnixiel

Incense: Ambergris

Office: This will aid you in besieging cities and destroying an area. It will also aid you in safe travel and creating peace between couples. It will get rid of things and is bad for sailors.

Meditation image: A fish in the sea.

Seal of Arrexhe:

Seal of the angel Amnixiel:

WORKING WITH THE MANSIONS OF THE MOON

Meditation

Let us wait until the moon is domiciled in the mansion that we wish to work with. Then in the Luna hour and with incense relevant to the work we can simply light a candle and place it upon the seal.

Perform a simple invocation unto the energies of the mansion and imagine that you are walking into the scene which is associated with each of the mansions. We can explore the mansion at this level and perhaps get a better understanding of their energies should we wish to work with them. Close the working with thanks for their aid.

Candle magic

When the moon is domiciled in the mansion consecrate a candle in the God Name and archangel of Luna and dedicate it to the angel of the mansion. Light this candle stating your intent and let this be in the Luna hour. See in the candle flame your will coming to pass.

This work can be repeated when the moon is again traveling through the mansion or at the next Luna hour, if possible whilst she is still in the mansion. Repetition will strengthen the working, making success far more likely.

Talismans

A: In the Luna hour draw the seal when she is in the mansion you wish to work with.

B: Create your circle using the names relevant to Luna to fortify it as previously shown.

C: Let the seal be consecrated as we have done before.

D: Make an invocation to God for the success of the work.

E: Invoke the power of the moon by using the Luna invocation and the Luna hexagram. Invoke the God Name, Archangel of the moon and the angel of the mansion that they may make your will manifest accordingly.

F: Hold the seal in the rising incense smoke as you make your call to the energies of the mansion you are working with and see your will coming into manifestation.

G: Give thanks to the energies invoked.

H: Close the ritual.

Such simple works can bring surprising results, particularly when they are repeated as the working is then reinforced each time.

LUNAR INVOCATION FOR THE MANSIONS OF THE MOON

For thee I invoke O Holy Mansion… (state mansion)
In the Mighty Name Shaddai El Chai
Who art the Living God
That by the power of the Holy Archangel Gabriel
The…(mansion) and the powers thereof
May attend unto my holy will.
Therefore, O Ye…(angel of the mansion)
Hear Me!
For I invoke thine aid that…(state intent)
By these Mighty Names.
SMIB.

DECONSECRATION OF TALISMANS

At some point you may wish to deconsecrate your talisman when you feel that its goal has been achieved. This can be quite simply done by waiting until the waning moon and burying the seal in the ground with the intent that the powers invoked will return to whence they came causing no fear nor harm to anyone or anything. Do not forget to thank those energies that you have been working with as part of your rite.

'As God hath granted thee access unto his storehouses
enter therein but wisely.'

Further reading

Greer. John Michael, Astral High Magic: De Imaginibus of Thabit Ibn Qurra

Greer, John Michael and Warnock Christopher, The Picatrix

Papus, Elementary Treatise on Practical Magic

Agrippa. Henry Cornelius, Three Books of Occult Philosophy

Thanks also to the psychic quester Charles Topham for introducing me to the art of etching metals.

Index

A

Abdizuel 113
Abra Cadabra charm, the 38, 47
Abrinael 125
Acarfa 113
Adriel 118
Agrippa, Henry Cornelius 96, 126, 132
Alahue 114
Albotain 101, 102
Alcalb 119
Aldebaran 105
Aldirath 108
Algarf 128
Algarfa 116
Algebha 111
Alheniel 128
Alichil 118
Almices 106
Almiquedam 127
Alnath 99, 100
Amixiel 103, 104
Amnediel 109
Amnixiel 129
Amutiel 120
Anael 80
Anaireton 25, 26
Anaphaxeton 25
Angelus 92
Annathra 109
Aquarius 59, 125, 126, 127
Aralim 64
Ardesiel 111
Aries 18, 96, 99, 101, 129
Arrexhe 129
Ataliel 116
Atarf 110
Athaya 107
Azariel 105
Azaruel 117
Aziel 126
Azimech 115
Azobra 112
Azoraya 103, 104
Azubene 117

B

Bacon, Robert 41
Barbiel 110
Bardon, Franz 24
Barrett, Francis 23, 24, 45, 46
Beni 88, 89, 90
Bethnael 122
Book of Oberon, the 48
Book of the Maccabees, the 45
burin 26

C

Caadacohot 125
Caadaldeba 123
Caaddalhacbia 126
Caaddebolach 124
Cancer 108, 109, 110, 111
Capricorn 59, 122, 123, 124, 125
Cassiel 57
chamomile 9
Chasmalim 68, 69, 70
Corpus Hermeticum, the 15, 56

D

Daath 76
Daniel 40
De Imaginibus 16, 24, 132
decans 18
Dee, John 10, 11
Dirachiel 107
Discoverie of Witchcraft, the 47
Doretheus 19
dragon 19, 113

E

Egibiel 119
Elbelda 122
Elohim 45, 46, 71, 73, 74, 75, 83, 84, 88, 89, 90
Enediel 101, 102
Ergediel 115
Exaula 120
Exodus 53

F

Fortune, Dion 15, 55

G

Gabiel 106
Gabriel 91, 93, 94, 95, 131
Geliel 123
Gemini 24, 39, 106, 107, 108
Genesis, book of 55
Geniel 99, 100
Gibor 71, 73, 74, 75
Glastonbury 9, 10
Greater Key of Solomon, the 24
Greer, John Michael 132

H

Haniel 80, 83, 84
Heh 45
Hod 45
Hollandus 6
Holy Ghost, the 40, 41, 42, 43
Holy Spirit, the 40, 41

I

Iah 25
Initiation into Hermetics 24
Ishim 93, 94, 95
Israel Regardie 6

J

Jazeriel 114
Jesus 21, 39
Junius 6
Jupiter 18, 19, 31, 32, 42, 43, 44, 66, 67, 68, 69, 70, 97

K

Kabbalah 6, 20
Kabbalistic 21, 45
kamea 12, 31, 34, 35, 96
Karmael 73, 74, 75
Kelley, Edward 10
Kharmael 71, 74
Kokab 85, 88, 89
Kyriel 121

L

lamen 79
LBRP 59, 60

Leo 10, 12, 18, 111, 112, 113
Levanah 91, 93, 94, 95
Libra 18, 19, 115, 116, 117, 118
Lilly 22
Llanyblodwell Charm, the 43
Luna 33, 59, 93, 94, 95, 96, 98, 130

M

Madim 71, 73, 74, 75
Magus, The 23, 45
Malakim 79
Mansions of the Moon, the 96, 131
Mars ... 17, 18, 19, 32, 35, 38, 71, 72, 73, 74, 75, 97
Mercurii, the 38, 41, 45
Mercury 12, 24, 33, 44, 85, 86, 88, 89, 90
Merlin 136
Mikael 76, 78, 79, 85

N

Nahaym 121
Nakhiel 76
Neciel 112
Nogah 80, 83, 84

P

Papus 17, 132
Paracelsus 6
pentacle 45
Pentagram 59
Peterson, Joseph H. 45
Philosopher's Stone, the 10
Picatrix, the 96, 97, 98, 132
Pisces 39, 127, 128, 129
Prometheus 56

R

Raphael 38, 39, 41, 85, 88, 89, 90
Requiel 124
Robert Cross-Smith .... See Raphael

S

Sachiel 66
Sagittarius 18, 39, 120, 121, 122
Saturn 17, 18, 19, 31, 35, 38, 41, 57, 58, 59, 60, 63, 64, 87, 97
Scheliel 108
Scorpio 19, 118, 119, 120
Seraphim 73, 74, 75
Shabatti 57

Shaddai 91, 93, 131
Shemesh 76, 78, 79
Spica 19
St Michael 50, 52
Straggling Astrologer, the 38, 44
Sun 10, 18, 19, 32, 34, 44, 51, 64, 76, 77, 78, 79
sword 45, 69, 74

T

Tagriel 127
Taurus 18, 19, 103, 105, 106
Tetragrammaton 45, 46
Thabit Ibn Qurra 16, 132
Theban 30
Three Books of Occult Philosophy 96, 132
tincture 9, 11
Topham, Charles 132
Traite Elementaire de Magie Pratique 17

trine 44
Tzadkiel 66, 68, 69, 70
Tzaphkiel 57
Tzedek 66, 68, 69, 70

V

Vau 25
Venus .. 18, 19, 33, 42, 80, 81, 82, 83, 97
Virgo 24, 39, 113, 114, 115

Y

YHVH ... 40, 45, 46, 57, 62, 63, 64, 76, 78, 79, 80, 82, 84, 87
Yod 25, 45

Z

Zamael 71
Zechariah 92

OTHER BOOKS BY GARY NOTTINGHAM

Foundations of Practical Sorcery - Collected Works (Unabridged)

A seven-volume set of unabridged magical treatises, of value to all levels of students and practitioners of the grimoire traditions, being based upon the work of a small group of occultists who have explored it in practice.

ISBN: 978-1905297856

Foundations of Practical Alchemy: Being a Prima in the Paracelsian Arte of Solve et Coagula

This work teaches the practical laboratory alchemy of the past masters and for the first time reveals many of their secrets, including the volatilization of the salts and the mysteries of the sal ammoniac salts. These are a major key to many operations of the arte without which the student fails in their operations.

ISBN: 978-1905297986

Ars Angelorum: The Book of Angels

A catalogue of seals and descriptions of 360 spirits who are ruled over by a series of archangels and angels. These are divided and assigned to the twelve signs of the zodiac. This grimoire provides a pathway towards self-discovery and direct contact with the angels who influence the various aspects of one's life.

ISBN: 978-1910191163

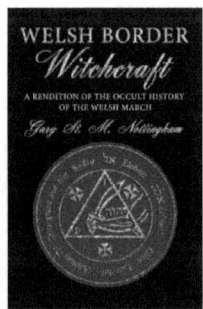

Welsh Border Witchcraft: A Rendition of the Occult History of the Welsh March

The occult history of the Welsh March is brought to life through stories of the cunning men and women, conjurors and healers, ceremonial magicians and witches who practised their arte in this liminal landscape, steeped in bloodshed and mystery, redolent of the spirit of Merlin, and where the mysterious Sin-Eaters practised their trade.

ISBN 978-1910191118

www.avaloniabooks.com

www.ingramcontent.com/pod-product-compliance
Lightning Source LLC
Chambersburg PA
CBHW032052150426
43194CB00006B/511